The Thespis in the Rest of Us

Your Guide to Realistic Acting

Kevin L. Meier

10 9 8 7 6 5 4 3
Printed in the United States of America

ISBN-13: 978-1468090055

ISBN-10: 1468090054

Cover art by Kevin L. Meier.
Internal photographs courtesy of Kevin L. Meier unless otherwise noted.

Title suggestion courtesy of Lauren "Lurn" Hutchison

This book is dedicated to the greatest love of my life, and through her belief in me, I was able to complete this work of art. I owe more to you, Baby, than I can ever repay.

TABLE of CONTENTS

Introduction

Picture an onion. A nice, juicy, Vidalia onion, handpicked from the market. You've likely heard this next part before. Creating a character is like peeling an onion. Just pull off layers of yourself until you've got the character you want. Sure this sounds great. And in some ways is partially true. Any character you create will come from within you unless you have the ability to change bodies (and minds) with people. The problem with the onion analogy is that even after you pull off layer upon layer of onion, you're still left with an onion. It smells like an onion, tastes like an onion, and will make you cry just as easy. And that's never a good kind of crying.

I prefer to look at the creation of a character more like a sand sculptor looks at the beach. He sees a nearly infinite amount of sand and with it he knows he can create a masterpiece. So he takes his shovel and begins to pile sand up. But he doesn't just pile sand upon sand. He prepares the sand. After he's thrown a few shovelfuls of sand into the pile, he takes water and pours it on. The water acts like a glue. Then he compacts it. He presses down and forces the sand into a tighter and tighter area and in this way the sand and water are bonded together and become strong. Then he does it again. Sand, water, compaction. Over and over. This may go on for an hour or two or more. Only after he sees the sand reach the size he desires, does the image within become clear. His hours of preparation have now brought him to the point of bringing forth life. So carefully, meticulously, he begins to scrape away the sand. He uses his shovel, a knife, a small scoop, a spoon, a brush, perhaps his hands, or whatever else his mind has devised that will allow him to fulfill his destiny as an artist. As an artist, he knows there are no set rules. Nothing can stand in the way of completing his art. So he continues to remove each grain of sand, slowly revealing what was hidden within that mound of sand. He doesn't skimp on detail. He doesn't rush haphazardly toward the finish line. He frets and ponders and fusses over his art until finally many hours later, it sits in the glorious sun on the windswept beach for the world to see. Yes, it is vulnerable. It won't last forever. The artist doesn't mind. He knows the wind and rain will someday batter it into oblivion. But for a brief moment it was his gift to the world. That is the glory of sand sculpting. Never again will that exact work of art exist. It was a one-of-a-kind piece, created out of love, specifically for that one day, in that one spot.

And so goes acting. Each time you step on stage and bear your soul, you bring a unique life into the world. But as hard as you may try, you cannot bring the same character to life during the next performance. Why would you? The joy of acting isn't in creating one character over and over. Joy comes from creating a new being each night so that the audience can experience through your eyes, a world full of adventure, intrigue, and passion. And through that, you have given the world a one-of-a-kind piece of art, created out of love. One created out of your soul.

Chapter 1

This Thing Called Acting

Like many of you, I started acting at a very young age. For me, it was at the tender age of five in my kindergarten play. And I haven't stopped since. More than forty years of acting. Sure there was some time off, but for the better part of that time, I've been involved in theater or film. Some of you may have similar stories. Some may have never stepped on a stage and uttered a single word. That doesn't matter to me. I don't care if all you ever do is play small roles in school plays or if you make it to Rodeo Drive and the lights of Hollywood. My job (I prefer passion) is to show you ways to make yourself the best actor you have inside you. Throughout this book, I'll give you exercises and explanations based on the Sanford Meisner Technique and share a few stories from my years on stage. Keep in mind that acting is a learning process. It should never stop. I am always looking for new books to read. But something I found lacking was a book that taught people the essence of realistic acting. And that's why I took on the task of writing this book. I have spent many years refining techniques through various exercises with thespians of all ages at my studio, Acting Up! Their willingness to throw themselves into my program has been nothing short of a God sent blessing. My thanks go out to all of them for the joyous hours we've spent together discovering our art. I love you guys!

I want to also mention a few people who have led me along this path. First to Mrs. Edith Cornett who in 6th grade, gave me the role that really propelled me down this life-long path. To my mother, who did such a fabulous job directing our church plays. To actor Kirk Baltz (*Dances with Wolves*), who first taught me what it means to commit as an actor. And to Larry Silverberg whose four-part series, *The Sanford Meisner Approach*, was so inspirational; it was from this that I adapted many of my exercises to meet the needs of the young actor. To my Production Manager, best friend, soul mate, and wife, Patti, for giving so much of her time at the theater. And to one of my best friends, Stanley. Your antics bring so much joy to the stage. Where would we be without you?

"Unless a man undertakes more than he possibly can do, he will never do all that he can."
Henry Drummond

How true that quote is. I am not going to tell you to cast aside your fears and plunge head first into this endeavor called acting. To proceed without first learning what obstacles lie ahead is a certain recipe for disaster. So embrace your fears. Use them to keep your head up, with your eyes and ears open. It's our eyes and ears that teach us about the world. It's how we learn what is safe and what isn't. It's where we learn new talents and how we learn to communicate. And it's what teaches us the art of acting.

As you study the techniques in this book, progress slowly. As much as I would like you to thoroughly enjoy this book and read it cover to cover in a day or two, I know that isn't the best way to absorb everything I've put into this book. Take the time to re-read, if necessary, each section. I've broken this book down into manageable sections that progress in a logical, easy-to-understand order. So, take your time and do each exercise fully. Don't skimp or rush the exercises. It's through these that you learn about yourself. And learning about yourself is where you can best learn how to act. If you ever have any questions about the material in this book, please contact me at the email address below. Seriously. I will make every effort to answer you via email or with a phone call. (So leave me your number.)

questions@actingupacademy.nct

As I mentioned in the introduction, creating a character is like building a sand sculpture. It takes preparation, care, and a vision of what lies underneath the surface. Every character you create comes from you. Nearly every new student tells me along the way, that they can't do something on stage. That it isn't something they would do. I say, "Good! Because that isn't you up there. It's your character." Everything you create lies within you. You have to remove those grains of sand that reveal the art underneath. But that doesn't mean you can just add whatever you think is necessary to create your masterpiece. If you haven't ever been mad or in love, then how do you have the foundation from which to become the character. You must prepare by going out and falling in love or getting angry. Go yell at something. Find an injustice in the world to be mad at. Watch a sunset and fall in love with it. You see, it doesn't have to be a person. Love and anger and passion come in many forms.

Once you've fallen in love with something, now you can use that to fall in love on stage. I bet you're saying to yourself right now about how there is no way you're getting up on stage and letting *that* happen to you. Remember, it isn't *you* up there. Sort of. It's the foundation you've created by experiencing the world. This gives you the opportunity to let your character experience those emotions. But to experience them yourself, you're going to have to make yourself vulnerable.

Be vulnerable? "Whoa, hold it right there", you say. "I don't think I can do that." Sure you can. You do it all the time. Every time you try something new or something that's out of your comfort zone, you're making yourself vulnerable. Ever strike up a conversation with someone you just met? Ever try something daring, like rock climbing or skydiving? Ever walk into a new school and feel totally out of place? We do it all the time. We all take that leap of faith and try new things. You made yourself vulnerable. And you survived. Same with acting. You step out on stage and try something new and foreign and soon you'll see that wasn't that hard. That doesn't mean it won't take work. But leaving yourself vulnerable and open to discovery every time you step out there to do a scene will get easier. I promise. In fact, I'll bet that it won't take long and you'll want to get out there, open up your soul, and experience the rush of acting. Yes, it's an addiction. But this is the good kind. It lets you see who you are. A vision into what makes you who you are. It opens up opportunities that no other art form allows.

So now you've made yourself vulnerable. You've opened your mind and heart and soul to what's going to happen on stage. Or at least you cracked the door open and saw that first shimmer of light. You are about to enter a new world. A world not so unlike the one you live in. The stakes are just as high here. Let me repeat that. THE STAKES ARE HIGH!!! In every play or movie, characters are going through life-changing experiences. They love, hate, grieve, desire, and every emotion in between. Because your character is real. They are alive. They exist. They have conflict in their life. They have a sense of urgency. You must believe they are real. You must treat them with the respect of a living, breathing human being. It is not enough to be on stage and just do what the script says.

Acting is not about doing.
It is about BEING, then DOING.

Other characters are counting on you. They need you to be emotionally committed to yourself and them. Yes, your character has something that motivates them. Some goal they are trying to achieve. But so does every other character. That's why the playwright put the character in there to begin with. Good playwrights do not have "throw away" characters. So no matter the size of the role, you as the actor must do all you can to prepare and then shed away all that is you until the character is revealed. Create that masterpiece. But don't do it for yourself. Do it for your fellow actors. Having a successful play is like being on a winning team. Everyone must work together to create something great. Give 110% in everything you do. And keep this one thing in mind. I call it our 1st Golden Rule of Acting:

Make your scene partner look good.

If you can do that and they can make you look good, then you'll have something great. I see it happen every time. We did an exercise with my advanced class the other night where I give out little slips of paper to each student. On it is a little backstory about their character. Not much. Just a sentence or two. Along with that is the essence of the scene. In this case, Philip enters through the door into the scene having just been shot in the stomach. There was a definite sense of urgency as he staggered into the room and collapsed on the floor. His scene partner, Andrew immediately ran over to see what was wrong. Here's the completely improvised dialogue that followed:

Andrew: Philip! Good God, what happened?

Philip: The gun went off.

Andrew: Oh, man. You're bleeding. We got to get you help. I'm calling 911.

Philip: It hurts.

Andrew: (on the phone) Help, please. My friend's been shot. He's bleeding real bad.

Philip: Andrew?

Andrew: Hurry. Please!

Philip: Andrew?

Andrew: Yeah.

Philip: I'm scared.

Andrew: I'm here. I'm not going anywhere. It's going to be ok.

Philip: It was an accident. I was just…

(Philip's body starts to shake. Andrew grabs Philip to keep him from banging his head on the floor. He places Philip's head in his lap.)

Philip: (groans)

(Andrew strokes Philip's head.)
Andrew: Stay with me dude. You're gonna make it. The ambulance is coming.

Philip: (groans again) Oh… I don't want to die.

Andrew: You're not gonna die. I won't let you. (beat) Come on buddy. We got a lot to do. You can't check out on me yet.

(Philip's shaking has slowed and his breathing has become very shallow.)

Philip: Tell Amy I love her.

Andrew: I'm not going to do it. You are. We're getting you to a hospital and you're going to be fine.

Philip: I don't know…

Andrew: Don't you give up on me!

(Philip's body has stopped all it's shaking. There is a long pause.)

Philip: Andrew, are you there?

Andrew: I'm right here.

Philip: I can't see anything.

(Philip dies and his body goes limp.)

Andrew: NO!

(Andrew immediately begins performing mouth to mouth resuscitation on Philip.)

And scene!

A perfect example of how Andrew's immediate reaction to Philip when he entered set the scene in motion. As the scene progresses and Philip approaches death, the urgency builds. As Philip realizes his death is imminent, his conflict of being scared about dying evaporates, but is replaced by Andrew's frantic pleas for him to hang on until help arrives. On review of the scene, Philip didn't preplan dying. He simply fed off Andrew and let the scene lead itself. Likewise, as Andrew saw Philip dying in his arms, his passion to keep him alive provided him with all the emotions that accompany watching your friend die. In fact, Andrew's CPR attempts were so spontaneous that he didn't realize he was doing it until I yelled "scene". Even Philip had no recollection of Andrew even doing it. This is what it means to "BE" the character. A couple notes about this scene. There wasn't a dry eye in class from anyone. Male or female. Myself included. The girls sitting next to me had such a death grip on my arms, I thought they might cut the circulation off. And for the record, Andrew and Philip were only 14 and 13 at the time they did this scene. Realistic acting doesn't have to wait until you're an adult or even an older teenager. You can do it now regardless of your age. And the rest of this book is going to show you how to do that step by step.

"You can't cross the sea merely by standing and staring at the water."
Rabindranath Tagore

So if you're ready to take the plunge, go ahead and turn the page.

Chapter 2

Rules of Acting

Wait a minute! Rules? Shouldn't acting be inspirational and free flowing? Yes and it will be. But first we need to lay down some ground rules. Don't worry, they aren't hard to remember. We can sum up this entire book in just three words:

Listen
Believe
React

Yep! That's it. Those are my three main rules to acting. Of course, it is more complex than that. Learning how to listen, beginning to truly believe your character is alive, and training yourself to not act, but react to what happens on stage takes time. In fact it takes years. But they are years filled with wonder and amazement. But it takes commitment. It takes discipline. And it takes a willingness to make yourself vulnerable. And if you obey these three rules and learn how to apply them to your acting career, I guarantee that you will have all tools you need to be a successful actor.

Every year at my studio we start with the first one, *Listen*, and progress from there. So let's spend this chapter just listening. At the studio, we spend weeks just listening. But not just with our ears. Sure, we start first with our ears but then with the rest of our senses. Like your eyes. "My eyes?", you ask. Well, yes. Listening means you are open to everything happening on stage. My father used to say, "You learn a whole lot more about people from listening than from speaking." And he was right. He was a master of observation. Within minutes he could tell you more about a person than they knew about themselves. His ability to read body language, speech patterns, and if close enough, their scent and skin texture. All signs of what makes up a person's behavior. As I grew older I began to take what my father taught me and apply it to my acting. Many times, I would just go and sit in a crowded spot and observe. Many of my multitudes of characters and behavioral characteristics came from my observations. Listening became the beginnings of my preparations. (We'll discuss preparing for a role in more depth later.)

When being interviewed on *Inside the Actor's Studio*, James Lipton asked Harrison Ford what was the most important thing to know about acting. He replied, "Listening". But listening goes beyond just using our ears. It applies to all our senses. Sight, smell, touch, and taste can all tell us what is happening on stage. The body and mind should be receptive of everything happening on stage. Even during monologues, you must "listen" to what is happening on stage. No matter how much preparation you've done to prepare for this role, things change. Listening is your greatest asset to help you cope with the constant changes that occur during any performance. And remember to be receptive to what your body is telling you.

"Listen and attend with the ear of your heart."
Saint Benedict

During class, all my students work on exercises to enhance their senses. We work on touch, smell, taste, and sight in addition to hearing. The first game we play is "Rock". Everyone sits and then "freezes" in place. They become rocks. Unmoving. They are allowed to do only two things. Blink and breath. My studio used to be co-located with a dance studio, so noise was the norm. We became so accustomed to it that we neglected the other noises around us. The students spent about 5-10 minutes just sitting and listening. Suddenly those unheard noises now sounded much louder. The individual tap, tap, tap, of the dancers shoes on the floor. The teacher's voice commands to her students. The breathing of the person next to you. Your own breathing. Maybe even a rumbling in one's own stomach. But what gets them the most, is the ticking of the clock. They would never hear it until they perform this exercise.

EXERCISE: Take 10 minutes and just listen.   Sit somewhere and freeze. No movement whatsoever Now listen for all the sounds you've been missing. Then write them in the space below.

_____

_____

_____

_____

_____

_____

_____

_____

_____

_____

_____

_____

_____

_____

_____

_____

Finished? Good. Try this from time to time when you're out in different environments. Train your ears to not just hear, but to listen.

But what about the other senses. Well, believe it or not, I've got exercises for that too. In fact, I've got a couple just for your eyes. But we'll get to them later.

A picture is worth a thousand words. But only if you really "see" what's in the picture. Just like the listening exercise, you have to stop what you're doing and focus on what you see. Take five minutes and spend time looking at a painting. Every minute or so, move in closer. Notice how different details come into view. Look at the brush strokes. Then the fine details of the brush strokes. I'm reminded of the scene from *Ferris Bueller's Day Off*, where our three heroes head to the museum. They stand before a very large painting and the camera progressively moves closer to the painting. With each jump, new details emerge until finally we see the smallest of details laid out on the very texture of the canvas. It's with this type of attention that you can truly see the beauty of not only art, but the world.

"The journey of discovery is not in seeking new landscapes, but in having new eyes."
Marcel Proust

Go to your library and find a book about art. Close your eyes and open it to any random page then open your eyes. It doesn't matter if there is a picture on it or not. Even a blank page is ok. Catch the first thing about it you see and shut the book. Don't linger and search for something. Just go with the first thing that caught your attention. What was it? Was it an object or a color? Was it in the center of the page? Do it again. Find a different picture and see the first thing that pops out at you. Do it a 3rd, 4th, and 5th time. Are you always seeing something in the middle of the page or is your peripheral vision hard at work? Now let's leave the book for a minute. Look straight ahead and notice the first thing that comes to you. Was it a big object or something small? What is a tiny detail that you saw? Use this exercise several times a day. Watch as you begin to see the smaller details in life.

Let's go back to the book. Again open to any random page. Now look at it. Don't look at anything else around you. Not a table or desk or a person near you. Just focus on the page before you. Study it. Take in the details. Spend a few minutes with it. Now mark down the page in the book and shut it. Write down as much about the picture as you can.

EXERCISE: Detailed observation of the page of a book

_____

_____

_____

_____

_____

_____

_____

_____

_____

_____

_____

_____

_____

Now let's bring this exercise into class. Pick a partner. Preferably someone approximately your height. Both of you walk up on stage. Once you're up there to your back to them. Their job is easy. They just have to stand there. Now turn around quickly and say the first thing you notice about them. Whatever it is. It could be their hair, eyes, glasses (if they wear them), clothing, jewelry, whatever. There is no right or wrong. But be specific about what you see. Don't just say "eyes". What color are they? Are they wide open? Blood shot? Be specific. In fact, start training yourself in specifics. You'll need it a lot in future exercises. Now have them turn around and when they're ready, they can turn back and notice the first thing about you. Now swap partners with somebody else and keep this exercise up until you've worked with as many people as time permits.

Did you start to see more details? The hidden things about people? Keep this up. Practice it on your own while walking down the street or through the mall. It's fun and no one will know you're even doing it.

"To think creatively, we must be able to look afresh at what we normally take for granted."
George Kneller

Let's do a similar exercise as the previous one, but let's use our fingers. Touch is important. It can be comforting. It can be informative. (Ever burn a finger?) Grab a scene partner and go up on stage. Stand facing each other. Now reach out and touch something on them. A hand. Their face. A piece of clothing. Feel the texture. Formulate how it feels to you. Soft or rough. Warm or cold. How does touching it make you feel? When we use touch, we step inside someone's personal space. It can be unsettling for the person being touched and for the one doing the touching. But it's a necessary part of acting. Somewhere along the way your character is going to need to hug or punch or maybe even kiss another character. Don't worry. It's not that bad. And a lot easier than you think. Remember our talk about being vulnerable earlier? Once you step out and take a chance and let yourself be open to new experiences, you'll find that it was well worth the risk. OK, so you've had your chance to use touch as part of your acting. Now it's their turn. Let them invade your space. Enjoy it. Oh and after they've had their chance to experience something about you, give them a hug. Not one of those fake ones either. Make it a big bear hug!

This next exercise involves not only touch, but trust also. Unlike the standard trust exercise of falling into your scene partner's arms, you're going to be led around the room by your scene partner. With your eyes closed. Sounds simple, right? We'll see.

For this one you are going to use only your hands. In fact, just one hand. This scene is all about movement. No dialogue. Get your fellow students and tell them to place themselves randomly around the room. Take one student and make them your scene partner. Preferably someone you aren't exceptionally close to personally. In a moment, you're going to close yours eyes. But first place one hand straight out in front of you, palm up. Your scene partner will place their hand on yours. Don't curl your fingers so that they can pull you along. Here, they're going to lead you. Like any journey through a play, someone leads the action. If done properly, the other characters will follow. If they resist and force to be "pulled" along by the action, then the play suffers. Same here. Trust your scene partner to lead you around the room. Their eyes are open and they can see everything. They will take you on a random trip around and near the other students. Their goal is to make sure you don't bump into anyone or anything. Remember our Golden Rule - their job is to make you look good. And you must trust them to properly lead you. Close your eyes before you start and rely on the feel of their hand to guide you around the room. Feel how their hand changes directions. How it speeds up and slows down at different times. Don't hesitate as you walk. Move at their speed. If you're body leans to catch up, then you're afraid of falling or their walking way too fast. Hopefully, they'll slow down. And hopefully the other students won't try to trip you up. Watch out for them. They aren't the kind you want to be in plays with. Do this for a few minutes and see how easy it becomes. As your senses begin to learn and anticipate your scene partner's moves, your trust in them goes up. It becomes an almost surreal feeling to be led around the room completely visually blind. Now swap roles and do it again. Have the other students move around the room after your scene partner has closed her eyes. Keeping the obstacles random prevents you from memorizing and thus pre-planning your movements.

OK, let's do it again. But with a twist. Instead of using the whole palm of your hand, we're only going to use the tip of your index finger. Put your hand in a fist, and then stick out your index finger. Your scene partner will do the same. And using only the tips of your fingers, she is going to lead you around the room. It's very easy to get separated from them during this exercise. That's ok. Stop, keep your finger pointed out there, and let them come back for you. Remember this! It applies on stage as well. As scene partners, you have to be ready to help out a fellow actor if she gets lost. And they have to be there for you.

Did you finish both exercises? Good. How was it? Difficult at first, I bet. It's hard to trust someone when we can't use our sight. We are so dependent on sight that too often we let it control everything we do. But as actors, we have to use all five senses. Even smell and taste to some degree.

Hope you're ready to get really close to your scene partner now. I hope for your sake that they used mouthwash today. No, I'm kidding. We'll come back to this later.

For now, we're going to do a simple (in theory) exercise. Grab a scene partner and get close to them. Lean in and smell their shirt. What does it smell like? Perfume? Detergent? Dirty?! Can you distinguish the smell? Some students can't. But try. Smell it again and again, if necessary. Smell is a sense that's very powerful to us, yet we don't use it much in acting. But the memories of unique scents linger with us for years. Decades even.

I spent several years in the Navy aboard submarines back in the mid 80s. Occasionally when I walk into a room full of machinery I catch a whiff that brings back memories of my naval years. It isn't an oily smell or diesel fumes. It's a strong metallic scent that instantly throws me back to the days when I would first climb aboard the submarine. The emotions it brings out are very mixed. I'm proud of my days of service and the great times I had with my shipmates. And there is a sense of nostalgia that accompanies that. But it also brings back the memories of being away from home for months at a time and the dread of being separated from loved ones for so long. I think it's the perfect example of how complex emotions can be in life and how as an actor we have to bring this same complexity to our characters.

Rarely does taste play into your preparation for a role or into your performance, but occasionally it does. Here are a couple examples from my past that have affected my execution of roles.

The first took place while filming *Constellation* (with Billy Dee Williams and Leslie Ann Warren). I was playing an extra in an outdoor restaurant scene. I was seated at a table with a beautiful young woman and we were "on a date" as the 2nd assistant director put it. I do not follow the strictest or healthiest of diets and my "meal" consisted of a nice salad and beer. On set, you don't actually drink, so my "beer" was actually apple juice. Unfortunately I could care less for salads and apple juice. However, I had a role to play. And considering I was placed square behind the actors and in full view of the camera, I had to do my job. And I did. I did my preparation and tore away the grains of sand of me that doesn't care for either item. Fortunately for me, my scene partner was very supportive and spoke a lot of encouraging words during my attempts at eating and drinking. (Another example of our Golden Rule about making your scene partner look good.) So keep that in mind when you have an opportunity to help your fellow actors. Someday it may be you needing the help.

Now this example took an an aura larger than life itself. It was about two months later and I was shooting an indie film in Nashville, TN. A science fiction thriller entitled, *The Shelter.* My job was easy. I played Patient Zero. The carrier of the deadly disease. It was on the "flight" back to the United States that the symptoms and disease began to show. Some time in the makeup chair and some fabulous work from the makeup artist enhanced the veins on my face and arms. And then the fun began. We climbed aboard the plane to film the scene. After a short talk with the director about shooting the scene, we started. All I had to do was make it look like I was about to be sick. Well, I've thrown up enough times in life to know what it sounds like, so I let it fly. What a great start. Then it was back to the makeup chair for a little more enhancement. Then back on the plane. The director then informed me to ramp it up a bit more. I asked if he wanted me to really vomit. No, he had that taken care of. That's when one of the asst. directors came on board and handed me a cup. Now this wasn't some little cup. This was a huge cup and it was filled full. Filled full of Karo syrup, Nestle's Quik, and trail mix! This black goop with chunks was one of the most disgusting things I've ever seen. And the crew knew it.

They thought this was going to be funny. But I had the last laugh. Now let me say that this concoction is to say the least very weird tasting. It is extremely sweet - almost too sweet. But when you add the trail mix in, this stuff takes on a life all its own. Now, I didn't have to swallow the stuff. Just take a big gulp, hold it in my mouth, make the impending vomit sounds and then throw the chunky, disgusting mixture up into a barf bag. It was all I could do to not throw up for real, but I worked the scene and held off letting that stuff go as long as I could. And when I did, I really let them have it. The sounds were so real, the crew had to start looking for someplace to vomit themselves. Ha! Take that. A little tip here. When you have something disgusting like this to do, do it great on the first two takes so that you can get it over with. The great thing for me about this scene was how the actual taste enhanced my performance. It brought a real (and I mean real) sense of authenticity to the scene. So often we rely on our other senses, but this let me focus on the taste to develop a strong feel of my character's impending doom. And did I ever have to listen to my body. Both to control the horror of that "drink" and to use it to propel my emotional commitment to my character. I'm so thankful for the opportunity this gave me. Rarely do you get to experience something this unique.

Listening doesn't come by hearing or seeing or smelling the loudest or brightest or smelliest object out there. True listening comes from picking out the finest details. Listen to a fine piece of classical music and pick out each instrument. I challenge you. We all hear the cellos and flutes. But can you pick out the percussionist playing the triangle? But for an actor, listening is crucial so that you are aware of EVERYTHING happening on stage. That doesn't mean that this is your main focus. You must learn to develop these skills so that they come naturally without conscious thought. They must become part of your character's "life" skills, so that you can be ready to adjust to anything that happens on stage.

In the next chapter we're going to use our "listening" skills and learn how to "believe". This is our 2nd rule. We must believe that our character is real. And the best way to do that is to believe that we have become the character. It might be you up there on stage, but it isn't.

Chapter 3

I Am Sam, Sam I Am

Green Eggs and Ham

Sam I am, I am Sam, I am Sam, Sam I am. The classic opening lines from Dr. Seuss's, *Green Eggs and Ham*. Sam is not just telling who he is. He states his name with authority and conviction. There is no doubt to who he is. He *is* Sam. And just like Sam, so must you be when creating a character. You must step onto that stage and declare to the world who you are. It doesn't matter if you're playing someone just like yourself or perhaps some make-believe Ogre from a land far, far away.

My adult career has had me play characters as diverse as a four year old child who has begun to question his vary existence to a thirty-five year old church-going woman to a homeless man who died alone in a cold alleyway all the way to playing the devil himself and everything in between. I've gone on dates. Got a divorce. Had my wife die before me. I've carried on imaginary conversations with my long, lost brother. I was stabbed and killed while sitting on a toilet and once even hit and killed an innocent little girl who ran into the street to retrieve her ball. I have laughed and cried and screamed in anger. I have loved and hated and been hated. The list goes on and on. In my life I have been involved with well over 100 plays and more than a dozen movies. Every one of these took preparation, dedication, and most of all commitment. My commitment to bring life to the character. A life based on reality.

The audience wants to put away their disbelief and step into your world. It's why they (and us) go see a play or go to the movies. Let's face the facts. Our life is humdrum and boring. We want to spend time outside our own world and experience someone else's. Whether people know it or not, they are willing participants to our "game". The very essence of seeing a play is to "suspend disbelief." So for two hours, our audience is willing to believe that what they see is real. But to fulfill their wishes, we must be willing to carry reality to them. And the easiest way to do that is for you to first believe that you have become the character. That's right. You are that four year old child. You haven't seen the world from a teenager's perspective. Things are new. They are exciting. They bring fascination and intrigue. All of your preparation and hard work must be focused on stripping away everything that makes you up until all that is left is that energetic, curious young child. And that's what we're going to spend this chapter working on. You're going to take the lessons learned from our listening exercises and apply them and through that begin to see what it is like to transform yourself into a rich, interesting, and rewarding character.

Let's start with repetition. Go stand in front of a mirror. Now, look at yourself and say the first thing that catchers your attention. Is it something about your hair or clothes? Is something stuck in your teeth? Now say that one thing over and over. Go on. Don't change what you say. Say it over and over again. Sure it sounds silly, but keep going. Maybe it goes something like this.

1. "My hair is curly when it's long."
2. "My hair is curly when it's long."
3. "My hair is curly when it's long."
4. "My hair is curly when it's long."
5. "My hair is curly when it's long."
6. "Wow, my hair is curly when it's long."
7. "Wow, it really is curly when it's long."
8. "I didn't know my hair had grown so long."
9. "Wow, it looks really great when it's long."

What just happened? How did your talk with yourself go? Notice how in our example exercise how our actress said the exact same thing five times in a row She was listening to her own voice. Then without thinking she began to believe it. Her realization led to that first "wow". Yes, she changed her exact words, but only because she was reacting to what she was hearing. That's perfectly fine. Reacting to what you hear is what we want you to do. Notice the order it happened in though. First she listened, then she believed, then finally she reacted. That is the key. If you haven't done so, go stand in front of that mirror and practice.

Done? Good. How did it go? Easy? Hard? Did you feel foolish? Never fear. It does get easier. Let's move on and see an example of repetition between two people. Please keep in mind that this next exercise was just that, an exercise by two people playing characters. It is not meant to demean one of the students. Feel the emotion rise as you read the lines.

Annie: You are a spoiled brat.

Samantha: Yes, I am a spoiled brat.

Annie: Yes, you are a spoiled brat.

Samantha: Yes, I am a spoiled brat.

Annie: Yes, you are a spoiled brat.

Samantha: Yes, I realize I'm a spoiled brat.

Annie: Yes, you realize you're a spoiled brat.

Samantha: Yes, I realize I'm a spoiled brat.

Annie: Yes, you realize you are a spoiled brat.

Samantha: Yes, I realize I'm a spoiled brat.

Annie: And a big baby.

(She didn't even realize she hadn't properly done her "yes, anding...", but that's ok, because she was reacting to the emotion of the scene.)

Samantha: Yes, I'm a big baby.

Annie: Yes, you're a big baby.

Samantha: Yes, I'm a big baby.

Annie: Yes, you're a big baby and a spoiled brat.

Samantha: Yes, I'm a big baby and a spoiled brat.

Annie: And nobody likes you!

Boom! Annie realizes what she's done and breaks character. It was very emotional for her and she had reached a personal breaking point. That's fine as long as she AND you understand that she had only touched the tip of the iceberg as far as emotion goes. As you progress with your acting and as you grow in the emotional maturity of an actor, you will be able to capture the emotion of the scene and stay with it without breaking character.

Whenever you have a scene such as this one, make it personal by keeping it real. If you truly hear the words and fervently believe all you're hearing, then you've achieved your first major step toward genuine, realistic acting. Remember that you should never force the dialogue or the action. When you do, we can see it because you're acting. But isn't that the goal. Believe it or not, no! What we really want is for you to **React**... That is what we'll study next.

Chapter 4

To Act, React

Let's start off quickly with something boring. Here's a simple definition:

> **React**: To act in response to a stimulus in a particular manner: *Reacting to a shock by jumping; to react to the word "coward" with anger.*

This leads me to one of my favorite exercises, "Pinch and Ouch". And if you're wondering, yes, it is a painful as it sounds. It starts off quite simple. I have the students all line up side by side. Then I walk behind them and randomly do or say things to each one. Sometimes a pinch on the back or a tug on their hair or maybe I'll say something really mean to them. It's all designed to solicit a response. They don't know what I'm going to do or say, so they can only react instinctively. Many times, it's just a "hey" or an "excuse you". The key is that they listen and believe what I do is meant to inflict pain and suffering on them. Sometimes I surprise them however by doing something nice. It doesn't matter because this exercise is designed specifically to develop reactions. Now take it a step farther and conduct this exercise when you are "in character". We'll discuss it later, but suffice it to say that the reactions are more pronounced. Yes, I do believe we are on the right track to "making this real".

Act before you think - your instincts are more honest than your thoughts.

Sanford Meisner

Ever walk up to somebody and know something was wrong with them just by the way they were standing? Humans are very adept at subconsciously detecting body language. We use it all the time to help us say and do the right things. Sometimes we mess up and say the wrong thing at the wrong time. Ah, our body language perception has let us down. Body language isn't spoken of much in drama. Yes, we hear about making big stage movements and such so that the audience can see what we're doing. But little is done with body language. Remember our Golden Rule? **Make your scene partner look good.** Why not use body language to help your scene partner know what emotions you are experiencing?

It's quite simple really. All you have to do is **believe** you feel a certain way.

True story: with every new class I have my students sit down around the room. I tell them to smile. Then I walk around the room and tell each one whether they're really happy or faking it. They're body language gives them away. Those that are really happy don't necessarily have the biggest smiles, but they're body is relaxed. Their facial muscles are relaxed. Why? Because they believe they are happy. It is extremely important that you are aware of how emotions come from inside you and then work their way out. If you're mad or upset or excited, it all starts inside you at your core. From there it builds and moves through the nerves and muscles until it works its way out. The body responds physically to how it feels emotionally. So if you're happy, your body will show it. If you're mad, it'll show it. So if you want to learn how to react you've got to start with believing. If you don't believe your character is mad, your scene partner and finally the audience won't believe it either. Believe it and the body and mind WILL react realistically.

An actor has to burn inside with an outer ease.

Michael Chekhov

To help understand how feeling emotions works on stage, I use this short analogy. Let's say you're supposed to portray sadness. If you don't believe you are genuinely sad, you'll be acting from the "outside in". Your mind will tell your body to be sad. So what you have is just the shell of yourself as sad. Your insides aren't sad. They're everything but that. By consciously controlling your emotions, it is unlikely you'll be able to react to the environment around you. But if you work from the "inside out", by feeling the emotions with your heart and soul, then what you have is this. Your mind will believe it. Your body will respond. It's not just the shell of your body that's sad. It's your insides, your heart, your mind, your body. It's the WHOLE you that is sad.

You've surely watched movies and saw how well an actor portrayed a character. You could see how real they made their character, because they were devoting their whole self to the character. They were working from the inside out. This is what you have to do. Figure out what makes your character tick. What has happened to them that made them who they are? The more you know about them, the more real they will become. The more you will "feel" them. The more you'll be able to work from the inside out. But knowing facts isn't enough. You have to believe them. That's the real inside out secret. It is a cycle of knowledge and belief. Over and over. This is just like building a giant snowball. You start with a little snow, pack it tightly, add a little bit more snow, pack it, and then begin to roll it on the ground. As you push the ball the snow adds to it and it gets bigger and bigger. And as you push harder, it grows and grows. You twist and turn the ball and mold it into a beautiful, round snowball. When you're done, there's no doubt you created a giant snowball. So goes believing in your character. With hard work, care, belief, and dedication, you shape and mold it into a beautiful creation.

You are prepared to do the hard work, right? You do believe in your character? You are committed to your character? If you're just beginning, then probably not as much as you need to be. Don't worry, it takes time. You're probably wondering HOW to believe in your character. Ask yourself this… Who is your character? Write down who they are. How did they get where they are? Go out and discover your character. Scrape away all the sand from your sculpture and create YOUR character. Embrace them. Become them. **MAKE IT PERSONAL!!!** Make it real. Feel it in your gut.

I watch beginning and intermediate students as they work through two and three person scenes and I see them struggle to believe. Most of the time it's because they haven't devoted the time to build their character. They don't trust in their ability. When you're working in your acting class, don't worry about failure. You can't do anything wrong other than to not try. So give it all you've got. Go for it. Don't hold back. Trust in your ability.

Golden Rule #2
I will not regret the things I do when I'm on stage.
I will only regret the things I didn't do,
when I had the chance.

Combined with Golden Rule #1, you're ready to tackle that scene. Believe in your character. Give it all you've got.

Do you "feel" like you're the character? Do you see things with their eyes? When someone speaks, do you hear it with their ears? If you can say "yes" to that, then you are ready to react. You are ready to work with your character in ways that will bring life to them. Now is the time to stop using your mind and instead use your heart. The mind hinders us at times. The heart is spontaneous. It is genuine. It doesn't ever act out. It only reacts to what it feels. The heart feels every emotion. It lives in the moment. The mind tries to control the emotions. It tries to plan moments. As actors, we don't want to plan for what may be. We want to grasp the here and now for it is this moment in time that matters. Work with your scene partner(s). Listen to them. Let their words and actions enter your soul. Let them stir the emotions inside your character. Let your anger, sadness, exuberance, desire, and passion burst forth. Do you feel it? Are you like me and ready to get on stage and let your character live?

Now is when you use this new found emotional freedom to help your scene partner. Even though emotions for you come from the inside and work their way out, the opposite is true for how you "give" these emotions to your scene partner. Your reactions and responses are taken and "listened" to by your scene partner. They are an outward expression of what you feel inside. They in turn "belief" that what they see and hear is real. In doing so, they take these emotions and let them build inside them so they can react in an outward manner. They then reciprocate by their outward expression of emotions. Listening, believing, and reacting to each other. And the cycle continues for the entirety of the scene or play. This is our cycle of life.

That's the basics. Our first 3 Rules. Listen, Believe, React. Everything builds from those three simple rules. They are not all we need to know. They are simply our foundation from which everything else will be built upon. Now let's move on and learn some improv games, so that we can eventually combine it all into a complete character.

Chapter 5

The Filter

What in the world does a filter have to do with acting? It may be the most significant concept that will free you so that you may be able to fully develop as an actor.

In our lobby hangs a sign: "Characters only beyond this point. Please check yourself at the door." Every student who enters the classroom and theater areas passes this sign. It is a constant reminder that we do not want Susie or Billy on stage. We are only interested in the characters they can create. It's this filter that stops us from doing actions that might embarrass us on stage. It keeps us from projecting our lines with our "theater" voice. The filter is what makes us have stage fright. From an acting standpoint, the filter is our arch enemy. He is the antagonist in our hero's journey and if we don't defeat him our hero will fail in his quest. Our character, our hero is counting on us. The greatest gift we can give our characters is to breakdown that filter. We must destroy it and give up control to our characters and thus letting them be free to live life as they should.

You're probably wondering how you can create a character and then let them go without having control of them. That's understandable. This is where you need to have trust in your characters. You need to know that your characters can take care of themselves on stage. You need to know that they can do whatever they "need" to do on stage. Many times I hear young (and old) actors say they can't do something I need them to do on stage. It's always, "But I can't do that!" I say, "Good. Cause I don't want you to do it. I want your character to do it." You must always remember that it isn't you on stage. It's your character. We are humans with limited experiences. Most times, we have not personally experienced what our characters have been through. (Remember our backstories?) But our characters have been through it all. It's made them stronger sometimes. It's made them afraid at other times. Their "experiences" have made them human. You, as an actor, need to let them go so that they can live. Give them the power to be free of your control.

A Treatise on Free Will

I'd like to cover the concept of free will and its application to our characters. Unlike the predestination (or free will) discussions that people like to argue about, this is not about that. This is simply about creating characters that can go on stage, live in the moment, and remain completely free of our guidance or better yet, our interference. We cannot as actors allow our personal selves to interfere in our characters lives. It is imperative that we simply allow them to enter the room, free to react to what happens during their existence. We must remain mere spectators.

This sounds simple and I believe that over time it will be for you. But before that happens we (you will notice that I include myself in all I am saying here) must give life to our characters. This is done by first establishing a solid, extended back story for them. Furthermore, once that is established, then we, and only we, can set limitations for them. Perhaps limitations is an incorrect way to put it. Perhaps it would be best to say "rules of existence". Keep in mind that rules ARE meant to be broken. Example, you create a character who is firmly against the consumption of alcohol. Under no circumstances would they touch the stuff. However during the course of the scene, your character experiences something tragic, and in so doing turns to alcohol in a desperate effort to ease the pain. You as the "creator" cannot make this decision for them. If you have nurtured your character and provided him or her with their own set of "rules" to live by, then you must be willing to let them experience life too.

One of the miracles that comes with teaching acting is seeing the time when a student's filter finally disintegrates. It's almost as if you see it flow out of their body and disappear into thin air. Every time I see it, it is so profound that I am able to remember where it happened, even to this day. When it happens to you, you'll feel it. You'll feel the liberation and freedom that will come with it. It's like a weight is removed from you. The blinders are removed and you'll look at the world with a different view. When your day comes, please email me and tell me about it. At this point you no longer need to call yourself an actor. You have now moved to a higher plain. You are now a ReActor!

Chapter 6

The Other Rules

Rule #4 – The Director is Always Right

The director is the vision. They are guiding force that brings the play from words on a paper into a living, breathing entity. As actors, we MUST trust their judgment. That doesn't mean when simply follow blindly. Certainly as creative people we can offer suggestions to improve a performance. But we also must be aware the director has the final say about the play or movie and we need to give them the respect they deserve. Remember that we work for them.

Rule #5 – No talking!

This is the most broken rule I've witnessed in all my years of teaching. When you're not on stage, please don't talk while others are performing. You want them to be courteous to you, don't you? Offer them the same professional respect. Who knows, perhaps you'll see something from your fellow actor or actress that will inspire you to create a new character or maybe a little quirk to add to a character. And after the director yells "scene", wait to see if the director has a critique for his performers. If you have comments about the performance, raise your hand and be acknowledged before blurting out your analysis. Remember to be as courteous to your fellow thespians as you would want them to be to you.

Rule #6 – What happens in drama, stays in drama

This is my least broken rule. And in many ways, perhaps our most important. As an actor, I want to be able to do everything my character NEEDS to do on stage. As a human being, I realize I might do something on stage that might be a little embarrassing if everyone I knew had heard about it. People outside of drama rarely understand the emotions we are pouring out on stage. Even less are the actions our character may do on stage. Unless someone has stepped on the stage, they are not likely to understand what you do or why you do it. So I implemented a rule that stops all talk of what happens on stage once class is over. Talking it out with those who saw it is perfectly fine. But running home and posting it on your facebook© status cannot be tolerated. Your fellow actors need to be able to trust you. The only way that happens, is to keep what happens inside drama, inside drama.

Rule #7 – When you die, you're dead

Here's your scene. It's a 1920's speakeasy. (Not sure what that is? Go look it up.) You were invited to the birthday party of Mr. Genoa "The Big Pasta" Rigatoni. The party is going to include some gambling in his speakeasy. You did your preparation. You built a character. You dressed for the part. You entered the scene. You had a great time. A toast was made. Then something happened. The cops raid the speakeasy. Shots are fired. You're hit in the chest with three bullets. Your character did not anticipate this happening. You as an actor didn't anticipate this happening. So what do you do? React, right? You drop to the floor, mortally wounded. You're bleeding. Your life is quickly leaving you. No one has come to your aid and you die alone on the floor of the speakeasy. Now what do you do? The scene is still going on. The police are "arresting" people. Investigators are called in. Do you lie there and watch the action? Do you get up and move "out" of the scene? No and No!!! Your character is dead. Unless someone picks you up, you don't move. You are still in the scene. The cops may need to "identify" you. The investigators may need to draw an outline of you on the floor. In other words, you are still your character UNTIL the director calls "scene".

It is a common practice for us to have annual Gladiator Games each year as one of our long form improv scenes. Generally our "gladiators" come out in pairs and battle to the death. The winner moves on with the chance to win real riches. Yes, I give out monetary prizes, trophies, etc. The losers… well they die. When they die, they lie in their spot until Caesar (played by me) has others move them from the arena. And there they lay in a heap until the evening's games are done. Dying isn't fun. This has become a great motivation for my actors, because no one wants to spend an hour or more "dead". It sucks and you don't get any prizes.

Chapter 7

Living in the Moment

The best we can do is live our lives with enlightened improvisation — to be so self-aware and fearless that we can live fully in the present and redeem our every moment and every human connection.

Doc Jensen

Right here and right now. That is what matters. I cannot worry about yesterday. That is gone. I can't worry about tomorrow. Tomorrow never arrives. I can only worry about the here and now. It is the only thing that I can have control over.

Live fully - moment to moment- that is reality.

Sanford Meisner

When I am on stage, there is urgency. I don't have days and weeks to finish something. I have minutes at most. My character needs an answer now. I need to find a way to overcome any conflict and clear any obstacles in my path. Time is something I cannot waste. I must succeed at this moment. This urgency is what I use to maintain my focus on what is happening right there at that exact moment. I cannot let a moment slip away from me.

Sure we all try to prepare for what our next line is, but we can NEVER lose focus as to what is happening on stage at any time. What happens if someone skips a line? What if a prop didn't make it on stage? I would like to say that every play I've ever been in has been perfect. Every line hit. Every entry and exit exactly on cue. Every prop was precisely where it was supposed to be. But this is live theater and fallible humans are involved. In fact, it's our faults that make live theater so compelling. And what makes us so nervous about going on stage.

Let me ask you a question? Do you live your life by following a script each day? "That's silly", you say. Of course, it is. None of us can follow a script. We wake up a little earlier or a little later some days. We take a little longer shower sometimes. We choose the clothes we'll where that day on a whim. Or maybe we wake up to hear it raining and realize that we'll need to wear something a little different today. Some mornings we sit down and have a nice cup of coffee. Other times we run behind and do our best to grab a bottle of water and a donut as we head out the door. And we haven't even talked to anyone yet!

You can see from something as routine as our morning routine, that things happen to make us alter what we might have preplanned. Maybe we live spontaneously and just go with the flow. In any case, we're doing exactly the same thing. What we are doing is that we are reacting to the world around us. In other words, we're "living in the moment".

Why is this important to the stage? Because our lives are real. And so should be our performances on stage. I cannot stand actors who "act". It isn't real. It's a series of planned actions and emotions that they've convinced themselves must be done on stage to make a performance effective. This is where they couldn't be more wrong, because they have become programmable robots. Theater is alive. It is a living breathing being. And to let it live we must be able to let it change and react to everything that happens between the wings and below the lights.

Every little moment has a meaning all its own.
Sanford Meisner

Yes, you are fully prepared when you step on stage, ready to hit every cue and nail every line. But you also must be prepared to react to changes. You have to hear your fellow actor's lines. You must hear the emotion in them. You must see their actions. And to each of those you need to react as if they are the first time you have ever seen or heard them. Never, ever, ever assume that you know the precise emotion you are going to respond with. Instead LISTEN to what you see and hear and respond accordingly. Do this in every rehearsal and in every performance. Make each time on stage an original work.

Take for example this scene. You are playing some rich, stuck up snob, on stage alone, sitting, in your luxurious wingback chair when your scene partner, the butler Niles, enters with your cup of tea. All he's supposed to do is bring it to you, sit on the table beside you and exit. You give a half hearted thank you and he leaves. But instead, he trips, and the tea is spilled into your lap. What do you do? Give the same half hearted thank you? That wouldn't be reacting now, would it? A sarcastic thank you followed by an apology from Niles might work. More likely, you would yell at Niles for being such a buffoon. Niles should probably beg to keep his job and try to clean up the mess as quickly as possible. It all depends on the background of your characters as to how you should react. What happens if Niles successfully delivers the tea to you and exits? You pick up the cup and spill it on yourself. What do you do? If you're "in character" you won't have to think about it. You'll react appropriately. That is the key. Be in character, live in the moment, and react.

When we perform a new work, it is common for people to ask us which performance they should attend. I tell them "all of them", because each one is a unique work. I don't want 4 or 6 or 8 exact replicas. I want each and every one of our performances to be special, because that is how we keep theater alive.

Chapter 8

Improvisation

I'm not going to try and cover every improv game. There are dozens and dozens out there. Many great books have been written that teach improv to the level well beyond I will cover in this book. With that said, I will not ignore the basics of improv. It is the fundamental form we use to teach all of our acting classes. Meisner relied heavily on the use of improv to teach his classes. We do the same. That is why it is important to pause in our studies on learning how to listen, believe, and react and to now work on our improvisational skills. Mastering, at least the basics, of improv is crucial in your continued studies of what we call "realistic" acting.

Atop for a moment and think about how you go through your day. Do you realize you improvise your entire life? Sure you have plans, but how often are they thrown out of whack? What about conversations with family, friends, and even your enemies? Each conversation is a give and take. A "listening" to the other person and responding (reacting) through words and actions. That is exactly what we do on stage. We react to everything happening around us. We live in the moment. You've been doing it instinctively your entire life. Let's apply those instincts with some simple exercises and dive right into the fundamentals of improv.

Normally an introductory course in improv would start you with an exercise called "Yes, anding…" We will get there, but before we do, let's begin with a little word association. I want you to grab a partner. Go ahead. I'll wait... … … … Got someone? Good. OK, here it goes.

We're going to start with an object. Let's say an apple. It doesn't matter who goes first. But for our purposes, we'll let you go first. I want you to think of something related to apple. Got it? You were thinking "red", right? No? Well, let's say you were anyway. Now we want your scene partner to think of something related to red but not to apple. Something maybe like "crayon". Good. Your turn again. Think of something related to crayon, but not to red. You came up with "box". Very good. See where we're going with this. Let's see how your exercise played out. We left off with you saying "box".

Your partner: wood

You: pulp

Your partner: oranges

You: Florida

Your partner: The Keys

You: lock

Your partner: door
(OOPS! That doesn't work! Keys, lock, and door go together. Try again.)

Your partner: portal

You: videogame

Your partner: Call of Duty
You: soldier

Your partner: homecoming

You: queen

Your partner: drama

You: stage

And so on and so on it can go. We normally let it go until each person has said something 20-30 times. Don't be surprised when you first try this, if you find it difficult to think of things or regularly find yourself linking three objects together. All these exercises take time to master. Now go on and do this several times until you can quickly think of objects.

Got it mastered? Maybe not, but you've got a good handle on it now, right? If you don't, then stop right here. The next exercise does the same thing but is about 10 times harder. Now is when we start to "Yes, and…"

This exercise is done just like our one word association, except we're going to do it in sentences instead of a word at a time. We'll still use a single word to start us off and we'll proceed from there. The important thing here is to always start the first part of the sentence with "yes" and join the second half of the sentence with "and". Never, ever, ever, join it with "but". That's a negation and we never, ever, ever want that. (Well, at least most of the time.) But we'll deal with negating statements later. For now, let's return to our previous exercise. Just like before, we're going to start with some type of subject. This time we'll go with "vacation". We'll let you go first again. I want you to say a statement about your recent "vacation". Something like, "We went to the Bahamas on vacation." Now we want your scene partner to hear what you said, so they'll start with "Yes, you went to the Bahamas on vacation." But they aren't finished. They've got to add to it. So let's say they add, "and I wanted to go with you." Did you see how their sentence went? It started with "yes"

43

and was joined by "and", so that we ended up with, "Yes, you went to the Bahamas on vacation and I wanted to go with you." Your turn again. Just like our previous exercise, you want to think of something that relates to them wanting to go with you, but not to your trip to the Bahamas. Make sense? Perhaps this is your response. "Yes, you wanted to go with me and you chose to go to summer camp." Now let's see how the rest of this exercise might go.

Your partner: Yes, I chose to go to summer camp and I'm glad I went.

You: Yes, you're glad you went and you overcame your fear of water there.

Your partner: Yes, I overcame my fear of water there and now I'm training to be a lifeguard.

You: Yes, you're training to be a lifeguard and that's just like you to rush into something new.

Your partner: Yes, it is just like me to rush into something new and you should try this new restaurant I found.

You: Yes, I should try to this new restaurant you found but you know I only like pizza and hamburgers.
** *OOPS! That doesn't work! Don't use "but".*

You: Yes, I should try to this new restaurant you found AND you know I only like pizza and hamburgers.

Your partner: Yes, I know you only like pizza and hamburgers and that's all this place serves!

You: Yes, that's all they serve and we need to go right now!!!

And Scene!!!

Yes, we would normally let the scene go much longer, but you get the point. This is the essence of "Yes, anding…" Now we won't always be saying "yes, and" in our conversations on stage, BUT we will be thinking it. It helps us to avoid negation. Nothing wrecks a scene quicker than actors saying "no", "not", "won't", "can't" on stage. Here's an example without the "yes, anding…" added in.

You: You are the meanest person I know.

Your partner: I am not.

You: Yes, you are the meanest person I know.

Your partner: You're wrong. I am not mean.

You: Yes, you are mean. I can prove it.

Your partner: No you can't.

See how we didn't get anywhere? Six lines of dialogue and NOTHING happened. We went nowhere. All we saw was two people disagree. From an improv standpoint, this should never happen.

It seems weird, but take this same scene and by "yes, anding…" we can make it into a much more compelling scene and still get the point across that your scene partner doesn't see themselves as being mean. Watch (read) this:

You: You are the meanest person I know.

Your partner: Yes, I am the meanest person you know and you think everything I do is mean.

You: Yes, I think everything you do is mean and I have ways to prove it.

Your partner: Yes, you have ways to prove it and your so called ways are weak.

You: Yes, my so called ways are weak and they may surprise you.

Your partner: Yes, they may surprise me and that will be the day hell freezes over.

See the difference? Basically the same thing, but by "yes, anding…" we added great depth to the conversation and to the characters. What I want you to do now is to repeat this exercise over and over. Don't have a scene partner? No problem. You can perform this exercise by yourself. If people see you doing this while walking around the mall, they may think you're a little weird, but hey, we're actors. We're all a little eccentric.

I cannot stress enough the importance of "yes, anding" enough. You *CANNOT* cut corners here. If you are unable to properly "yes, and", you will not be able to effectively move forward with your acting skills. Spending the required time here will pay off handsomely later on. And don't think that just because you get it down that you shouldn't continue to work on it. Come back for refresher time every so often. I have all my "accomplished" actors and actresses work on this skill many times throughout the year.

After you feel comfortable with "Yes, anding…", it's time for us to move onto some other foundation building exercises.

Once you've learned how to properly carry on a conversation (improv style), it's time to start working on dealing with our on stage movement. Normally, in plays, actors have all the props they need to portray a scene. They have furniture to sit on or items to hold, but an improv artist doesn't have those things normally. We are forced to "create" all our own props. The great thing about that is that we can create anything we need. We fill an entire room with furniture. The key is to make sure we don't break the rules of making things magically disappear or that we walk through our furniture. We call this "Awareness of Space".

This takes imagination on your part. You've got to "see" everything around you. Here's what I want you to do. Look to your right. See the wall? Good. See the refrigerator against the wall? Good. What does it look like? What color is it? Which way does the door open? Now walk over there and open it up. Grab the handle and tug on the door. Did you keep your hand on the handle or did you let go? Doesn't matter. I just want you to know. Look in there and find a bottle of water. Take it out and open it up then take a drink. Did you shut the door to the refrigerator? Shouldn't you? Mom doesn't want you wasting electricity. What did you do with the cap to the bottle? Is it still in your hand? Did it magically disappear? I hope not. Now look to your right. See the table and chairs. Walk over there and put the bottle on the table. Did you tip the bottle on the way over and spill the water? Did you put the cap on the bottle before or after you set it on the table? Perhaps you threw the cap away. If you did, well done. That's adding to your awareness of space. Now I want you to drag that table out into the middle of the room. Move the chairs first!!! Got it out there? Good. Now go to the refrigerator, cabinets, pantry, or wherever to get all the "ingredients" you will need to bake a cake. Did you get all the pans you'll need? Did you open AND shut all the cabinet doors. As you went back and forth getting things, did you remember exactly where the table was? You didn't walk through it did you? Now mix all the ingredients together and bake that cake. After it's done, put some icing on it, cut yourself a piece and enjoy!

This is a simple scene to do because there's only one person involved. What do you do when there are 2 or more on stage? Not much really. You need to ensure that your scene partner knows where things are. And you need to know where they place items or furniture. This is all part of the "Listening" we worked on back in Chapter 2. Hearing AND seeing everything going on around you. Being aware of your space.

Building Blocks - The Foundation of Interaction

Every house, if it's going to survive, must be built a solid foundation. And so it goes with a drama troupe. Many years ago we were doing some warm up exercises in class and to put it simply, my students were not focused on anything other than talking to each other. I am a firm believer in team dynamics and feel that every team should participate in exercises that build team unity. So to get the kids focused, I came up with a new exercise. Originally it didn't have a name, but it didn't take long for us to start calling it building blocks, because that's what it looks like. The first student comes out and strikes a pose. Then the next student comes out and "attaches" to the first student in their own pose. And so on and so on, until we have this great big group of students all attached to each other. Little did we know at the time that this would literally become the foundation for our improv troupe. Through the years, we've come to refine the exercise so that it accomplishes many things for us. First, it breaks down what we call "the filter". Beginning students fear physical contact with people they don't know. From a drama standpoint, physical contact is necessary to realistic scenes. Performing *building blocks* over and over allows each student to eventually work with every other student. We realize that physical contact isn't bad. In fact, it becomes a lot of fun to find new ways to attach to each other. We can attach with our hands of course. Or our arms. Then again, we can use our feet, legs, foreheads, elbows, noses, and even our backsides! And because we all know that everything goes, we build our trust in each other. And trusting your scene partner can't be stressed enough.

As students become more and more comfortable with each other, we then have them add to their specific building block. As they come out to attach, we want them to portray an emotion that is a REACTION to someone who is already out there. This allows us to build a series of vignettes within the overall scene (see picture).

This little exercise is so important to us, that we often use it at the beginning of our improv shows to get the audience warmed up and laughing. Explore this game to its fullest and see where it takes you.

Improv Games

The Machine

This game is similar to Building Blocks in that it involves the whole group working together. The objective here is for the team to work together to build a very special, one-of-a-kind machine. The first person comes out and does a repeatable activity. The second person comes out and adds to the activity. It doesn't matter what the movement is, but each successive person should add something to the overall machine. The parts don't have to be added in order but each activity should logically link. To add to this exercise, have everyone do it again, but this time each person does an activity AND adds their own sound effect. WARNING – This can get very loud. Once the group has mastered this exercise have them take it a step farther. This is best done when there is movement and voice. Just as before, have the group build the machine, but rather than calling "scene" at the conclusion of the build, instead, have the group disassemble the machine in the reverse order of how it was built. This helps them focus on their role within the machine and increase each performer's visual and auditory stage awareness.

Snap

Imagination… It is your friend. Use it. You'll need it here because we're going to play with an imaginary ball. You can do this by yourself, with a partner, or a whole group of people. Let's be selfish right now and just let you play with the ball. Place your hand out in front of you, palm up. Now "see" the ball in your hand. How big is it? What color? How heavy? Is it new or old? Now, I want you to bounce it like a basketball. Now you can't just bounce it like you would a normal basketball. The game is called "Snap" for a reason. So each time you "push" the ball down, snap your fingers and each time it comes up "catch" it with a snap. It should go like this. Down "snap", bounce, up, catch "snap", down "snap". Keep bouncing the ball. After you get the snapping down to the rhythm of the bouncing ball you're ready to move on. Now bounce it up against a wall. Bounce it off the bottom. Then the middle, then the top. Bounce it off the ceiling. Send it ricocheting into a corner. Did it hit something and stop? Go pick it up.

Now find a friend to throw the ball back and forth with. Go crazy with it. Throw it anyway if you want. Turn it into a big beach ball by "blowing" it up. Turn it into a bowling ball and "knock" someone over. Turn it into a cannon ball and "shoot" it out of a cannon. Find some more friends and have them join in. Play with the ball. Mold it into anything you want. Split it in half and throw two balls around.

Let me caution you here. It is vitally important that when you throw the ball at someone, that you make eye contact with the person you're throwing the ball to. They need to know it's coming so that they can catch it with a snap. You certainly don't want to hit them unknowingly in the head with a ball.

What are you Being?
This is the first true improv game that even the youngest performers can learn to do well. The first performer comes out and acts out an activity. For our purposes, let's say you are a dog washer. Remember to get the shampoo, a bucket (fill it with water), and a scrub brush. Once you "catch" the dog, start shampooing him. After a short period of time (10-30 seconds), the second performer comes out and asks, "What are you being?" It used to be called "What are you doing?", but acting is about being, THEN doing. Always make sure you are being the person BEFORE you do anything. Your job is to think of something completely different from washing the dog. What did you come up with? An astronaut preparing to blast off into space? Wow, we think alike! Now the second performer has to act out just what you told them to

BE. When the third performer comes out, the second performer will give them their own unique person to BE. This continues until all the performers have gone. But don't think you're quite done. Since you went first, you'll need to go out to the last performer and ask them, "What are you being?" They'll tell you who to be, but you don't have to be it, unless everyone is taking more than one turn at the game.

Freeze Tag

Show Them, Don't Tell Them!!! With few exceptions, nothing is more boring to watch, than to see two (or more) people on stage just talking. We don't come to the theater to watch people talk. We can go to a coffee shop and see that. We come to the theater to see movement! Action! Feats of Greatness! Thus, we have "Freeze Tag". The key to this game is movement. Lots and lots of movement. Engage with your scene partner. We'll need everyone on stage for this, but we'll begin with just two people performing a scene. Pick someone and jump out there on stage. Let's give you a scene idea that would involve movement. Maybe you're gladiators in training. OK, begin! The scene is off and running. You stretch a little to warm up your muscles. There's back and forth gossip about the newly arrived gladiators. Now grab your swords and begin to battle. You tease your opponent with a few short strikes of your sword. You strike and parry across the stage. Soon, you begin to dominate the battle and force your fellow gladiator to retreat. But they won't give up. They fight back. The intensity of the battle increases. Swords clash! The fight is on. A swing of your sword sends your opponent to the ground and their sword flying. You stand over your opponent about to strike the final "mortal" blow. "FREEZE!" yells a fellow student. You and your scene partner IMMEDIATELY freeze in position. The other drama student runs on stage, taps you on the shoulder, and assumes your pause. As you move to the back of the stage, a new scene begins with the two students on stage. But they are no longer gladiators. This is a new scene created from the positions they emerge from after the "freeze" position. Where it gocs is up to them. Hopefully they've chosen something full of action. Clumsy ballerinas? A father helping his son up after falling off his bike? An excited child trying to wake his parents on Christmas morning? The possibilities are limitless. Everyone should take turns yelling "freeze" whenever they see a great action to start from. Make sure you run out there and tap one of the performers out and assume their previous position as quick as you can. This is a high energy game that's a lot of fun.

Stand, Sit, Bend

You'll need three people for this high energy, action packed, and absolutely hilarious game. The premise is simple. You're going to do a scene just like you normally would. But in this case, one person must always be standing, one must always be sitting, and one must always be bent over. If anyone changes position, such as standing to bent over, then one of the other players must assume the standing position. Movement is the key to this game. Your scene suggestion should involve something with lots of movement, like workers in a ball bearing factory. The dialogue is important, but certainly plays second fiddle to the movements. You may want to consult a physician before performing this exercise, because when it is done right, it is an excellent aerobic workout.

Mood Swings

The premise of this game is just like Freeze Tag. Played exactly the same, except here we're worried about emotions. Each scene should have dramatic shifts of emotions. From "love" to "anger". "Despair" to "giddiness". Play with the emotions. Change them in every way possible. But with all scenes we do, make sure you are following our first three rules... Listen, Believe, React. Never, ever go out on stage and act.

Questions Only

The game is played with 4 people. Two in the center and two people who will stand behind the other two with one on each side of the stage. See the image below:

The game is played exactly as the title implies. You're going to carry on a conversation using ONLY questions. If a person doesn't use a question, starts with a sentence before their question, or can't come up with a question, they are "buzzed" out and the person behind them comes in and starts the conversation with their own question. This continues for as long as you want the scene to go.

There is a fun variation of this game called "Questionable Impressions". The players are still required to speak using questions only, but we add a little twist to it. Each player is required to use an impression of some character, such as a movie star (i.e. John Wayne), a cartoon character (SpongeBob SquarePants), a TV celebrity (Tim Gunn), etc. Or, if you're really bad at impersonations, and as a last resort, you can use a foreign accent. The key is to use any voice that's not your own. You don't have to change accents with each line, but you do have to change characters each time you come out to do lines during the scene. The fun in this version comes from seeing people epically fail in their attempts to impersonate characters.

Hitchhiker

Speaking of impersonating characters, Hitchhiker is all about that. The fun here is that you can say and do anything you want and your scene partners have to do the same character you do. To play the game, it takes at least three people, but generally this is for a much larger group. So once your group is assembled, grab three chairs and assemble them like the illustration below.

Player one starts off and walks over to the "car" (being played by the chairs) and opens the car door. (Remember our awareness of space?) The player steps in, sits down in Chair #1 (Chair #2 for our British friends), grabs the "steering wheel", and starts driving. Soon, a hitchhiker (Player 2), with thumb out, appears outside the passenger side of the car. The driver stops, the hitchhiker enters the car (don't forget to open and close the door). Immediately, they begin to portray a character of any kind. It doesn't have to be an impression of some celebrity or TV character. It can be a pregnant lady, an opera singer, a mime, or whatever you can think of. The possibilities are endless. Once Player 1 sees what Player 2 is doing, they are forced to portray the same character. This game isn't about reacting. This is about duplicating. There is still the "yes, anding…" to do, but don't portray a different character. After 5-15 seconds, Player 3 appears as the hitchhiker and flags down the car. They enter the car and take Seat #2. The Player who was in that seat moves to Seat #3. Player 3 portrays their character with Players 1 and 2 trying their best to duplicate Player 3. After another 5-20 seconds, a 4th player appears and flags down the car. Now the musical chairs begin. Player 1 exits the car. Player 2 takes over the driver's seat. Player 3 takes over Seat 3 and the newest player takes over Seat 2. And the game continues. Players exiting the car go to the back of the line and wait their turn to enter the car. This game can continue for as long as the players can come up with fresh characters. It's ok to rotate the group waiting in line so that the same players aren't in the car at the same time. Be creative with this game. Try as many crazy ideas that you can. You might surprise yourself.

Use this game frequently to encourage the development of new characters. This is also a crowd favorite during improv shows for its fast paced action and rapid fire snippets of comedy.

90 Second Alphabet

This is a wonderful beginning improv exercise for three people. You can use four, but we've found three to work best. Obviously it's very short since it's only a minute and a half long, so you can practice this one several times during a class session. You'll need a scene suggestion as always. For our exercise, let's go with "Lewis and Clark are trying to convince Sacajawea to help them explore the Pacific Northwest". But don't start yet. We haven't fully explained the game. We need someone to give us a letter of the alphabet. From the back, I heard someone yell "F". Now to play this game, the first sentence will start with the letter "f" and each successive sentence will start with the next letter of the alphabet. You'll have 90 seconds to go completely through the alphabet and return to the letter "f". There is no time to waste on stage. Dialogue needs to flow quickly. And don't forget throwing in your actions. Don't be discouraged if you don't meet the 90 second timeline. You'll get faster each time until you can actually perform this in well under 90 seconds. Here's a sample start for you:

Player 1: (Yelling to an unseen worker) Finish packing those supplies!

Player 2: Get my maps too!

Player 3 (Sacajawea): Hello gentlemen.

Player 2: I'm Lewis.

Player 1: Just finishing up the final preparations.

Player 3: Knives… you'll need lots of them.

Player 1: Lewis took care of that.

Player 2: Maybe you should go with us.

And so on and so on until the last sentence starts with the letter "f" or whatever letter you chose to start with. Don't let anyone skip a letter. Call them out for that mistake. The fun will come from watching the players struggle with their alphabet.

When you get really good at this, try it backwards. Both the alphabet AND the scene. Yes, you can perform the scene backwards, but this only for accomplished improv artists.

Song titles
Perhaps you've watched episodes of "Whose Line is it Anyway" and seen this game played. This one isn't for the feint of heart. It requires very good "Yes, anding…" skills in addition to a vast knowledge bank of song titles. The

game is played with 4 people, set up just like Questions Only. Two in the center who will engage in a conversation that uses only song titles. The remaining two people stand behind the other two with one on each side of the stage. If a person doesn't use a song title, or can't come up with one, they are "buzzed" out and the person behind them comes in and starts the conversation with a song title. This continues for as long as you want the scene to go. A tip for you... Start with a song title that establishes a connection between the two people on stage. Here's a little sample:

Player 1: Hey there, Delilah!

Player 2: (A nod of the head.) Angie.

Player 1: (Looking up.) It's raining men.

Player 2: (Shrugs.) Who'll stop the rain?

Player 1: It never rains in southern California.

Player 2: Only God knows why?

Does that make sense? I hope so. If you're new to improv, this can be hard to master. It's a great game to play because you can watch even the better improv artists struggle with it.

Movie Titles
This is a game I developed on a whim one night. You would think Movie Titles would be just like Song Titles, but I didn't want it to be quite the same. Yes, you'll use movie titles in your conversation, but with this one, you incorporate them into a sentence. You'll still need four people to play and you'll line up just like our other four person games. Here's an example for you (I've put the movie titles in **bold** for you.):

Player 1: I'm leaving for **Casablanca** tomorrow.

Player 2: How long before you'll be **out of Africa**?

Player 1: At least **9 ½ weeks**.

Player 2: Maybe your next trip will take you to the **forest, Gump**.

Player 1: They can't send me to the forest! I'm a **star. Wars** WILL be started if they try.

Player 2: Oh yes, it would be a **war of the worlds**.

This is a crowd favorite and one of the funniest games we play. Play with it. Give it a go. Explore wherever it takes you.

These are certainly not all the improv games we play. In fact, we've barely scratched the surface of all the games we use in class, in rehearsal, and during our improv shows. There are many great books out there that specialize in improv games. I would suggest you find one and try out the ones they suggest. If you'd like to see how we play some of these games and many more, check out our YouTube site.

actingupacademy.youtube.com

Short and Long Form Improv
In Chapter 17 of this book you'll find a section of scene starters. These are used to assist you in what we call "short form" and "long form" improv. Unlike the games we covered earlier in this chapter, these are scenes to help you develop the ability to listen, believe, and react. They will also help you create interesting and compelling characters.

In "short form" improv, the objective is to build and create a single scene based on an idea or suggestion. They can run from less than a minute to well over 10 minutes depending on the complexity of the scene. This isn't difficult to perform. The key for you is to immerse yourself into the character. There is no time to work your way into the character. Most scenes of this nature involve 2-4 people, but some can be done solo or with as many as 8-10.

Got an hour or more and want to try something really fun? Give "long form" improv a chance. In long form improv, the idea is to interconnect several "short form" scenes into a full and complete story. This is best done with an ensemble of players, but I've seen it done with as little as 4 players. You'll need several ideas to start a long form scene and there are two simple ways to kick start the scene. First, you can try "Person, Place, and Thing". They don't need to be related. It's actually better if they aren't related. Something like this:

> Person: The first man to set foot on Mars
> Place: A church
> Thing: An egg beater

Start with two players on stage. They should work toward creating a scene that utilizes either the person, place, or thing, but not two or more of them. This scene should not work toward a conclusion. It should work toward a nice plot point that creates a natural pause. Many times this pause is at a crucial juncture in their story. This will leave the audience wanting more and they'll anticipate this scenes continuance later. Now a second set of players comes out and performs a scene with either the person, place, or thing that the first team didn't use. They shouldn't make a conscious to tie their scene in with the first scene, but if it happens that's ok. When they reach a natural pause point, call "scene" and send the third team out. They should use the last of the person, place, or thing that hasn't been used yet. Now once they reach their pause point, it is up to the remaining players to decide when they need to come on stage and continue their scene. It is perfectly ok to use more than three teams to tie the story together. It is also perfectly fine and DEFINITELY desired to see players play more than one character. There is no limit on the number of characters people can play or the number of scenes needed to complete the story arch. As the scenes progress, the players should start to find common ground between the scenes so that all the players can see where the story is headed to. This takes time to master, but when done correctly is perhaps the most fulfilling form of improv.

Another way to start a long form scene is to use "One Word Association". Start with a common idea, such as a garden rake. Using the one word association we described earlier, build a series of approximately 20 ideas.

Garden rake, work, money, college, freedom, slavery, Africa, Mt. Kilimanjaro, hikers, lost, TV show, film, shower scum, wash, car, race, Tour de France, steroids, doctor, and Dr. Seuss.

Once you've reached that point, start your scenes and see how many of the 20 ideas you can incorporate into the complete story arch. Unlike "Person, Place, and Thing", you can use more than one idea in the opening scenes. You can use people and places related to the ideas. In some cases, you may not remember or be able to work all 20 ideas into your scenes. That's ok. The key is to have fun and run with the ideas you can.

Chapter 9

Creating the Character

What we want is character, and this nobody can give us. It is a thing we must get for ourselves...

It is gained by toil -- hard toil. Neither the sympathy nor the generosity of our friends can give it to us... It is attainable; but we must attain it, and attain it each for (ourselves). I cannot for you, and you cannot for me.

Frederick Douglass

Life can only be understood backwards; but it must be lived forwards.

Soren Kierkegaard

How do you create a character? I've been asked that question more times than I can count.

It's going to take some work. Be prepared because if you want to do it right, then it's going to take some serious research on your part. You're going to need information. And lots of it. So to start, read our scene and then ask yourself these five questions:

Who am I?
What did I do to get here?
Where am I and where have I been?
When did this occur and when did the events leading to it occur?
Why did I do it?

After you ask yourself each question, ask it again by adding "Why am I who I am? Why did I end up where I am?" And on and on.

The Scene

You have been incarcerated (imprisoned) in Chiblanka Prison in the isolated country of Krakistan. You are on Death Row. You have killed one or more persons. You are guilty of your crime. It is the policy of the prison system to execute inmates without warning on Tuesday evenings. You do not know which Tuesday you will be executed. You just know that you could be executed any time after 5:00 each evening. Methods of execution vary, but include hanging, gas chamber, lethal injection, firing squad, and electric chair. Executions are generally conducted in front of the inmates. There is no chance of escape except through death. And there is no chance of being pardoned for your crimes. The justice system is harsh in Krakistan. Men and women are housed separately but brought together each evening after dinner. This is the time of socializing. Occasionally, the guards will sneak in snacks if it is someone's birthday. Sometimes a cake is brought in for the inmates to share. The guards risk arrest if caught smuggling items. Is today your day to die or will you live at least one more week? How many Tuesdays have passed you by so far?

Write your character's backstory in the space below.

_____

_____

_____

_____

_____

_____

We must all be vigilant in our efforts to thoroughly prepare each week for class. This does not mean that we must spend long periods of time writing details of our character onto paper. For some that is what they do. For others like myself, I spend the week forming the details. As different items enter my conscious, I evaluate them and decide whether that is how my character will live by. It is the continuing process of using some and discarding others that allow me to build my character. As the week progresses, my understanding of my character grows. I begin to see the world through his eyes. I see what he wears. I hear his voice. I have been known to spend days or even weeks speaking as my character, regardless of any accent or vocal quirks. (This makes for an interesting home life with my family.) Use whatever means necessary so that when you breathe life into your character, with it comes absolute and utter free will.

Achieving your Character's Potential

If you want to achieve your character's full and complete potential, you MUST, I repeat, MUST BE THE CHARACTER. You cannot be the shell. You cannot be mostly the character. Acting is not about doing. It is about **BEING**, then doing. If you insist on doing first, then it will be YOU doing the actions and not your character.

> **You are not meant for crawling, so don't. You have wings. Learn to use them, and fly.**
> Mevlana Jelalu'ddin Rumi

Your character's full potential is their destiny. It is their dream. You cannot simply leave them to fend for themselves. You are the gardener of your character. You have been given the task of nurturing them. Feed them, water them, love them. Understand this. We are not talking about being the best. We are talking about achieving the FULL POTENTIAL of our character. Like us, characters are not without their flaws and self-imposed boundaries. It is our job to help them overcome anything that can slow them or stop them and make them the best that they can be. You can help them achieve this by following a few simple guidelines.

1. You need a roadmap. You might find your way by walking aimlessly, but you'll save time and energy by following a simple path. Search out where your character needs to go and build a map for them.

2. Do not listen to others tell you your character can't do something. This is an obstacle they are setting for you. Besides they don't know the journey you're on.

3. Push your boundaries. Stretch the limits of the situation your character is in. You don't know how far you can go until you go beyond where you've been.

4. Be curious and use your imagination. Fascination breeds intrigue. Don't worry about the end result, but rather the journey. This is where new eyes are found.

5. Your character's potential may have no limits. Don't assume that once you have overcome an obstacle or achieved a goal that you are done. Set the bar higher and go for it!

We don't live for realities, but for the fantasies, the dreams of what might be. If we lived for reality, we'd be dead, every last one of us. Only dreams keep us going...When you are acting, don't settle for anything less than the biggest dream for your character's future.
Michael Shurtleff

I've included a list of emotions. As you begin to create characters, use this list to assist you in finding the strengths and weaknesses of your characters. In particular find opposing emotions that will create internal conflict within your character. This internal conflict often does more to help a character grow than any external conflict they will encounter.

My college studies introduced me to psychologist Abraham Maslow. I didn't know anything about him before that first college course and it's not that I've studied everything he's written. But what he did develop was his Hierarchy of Needs. Not only does it apply to us as humans, but I found that it equally applies to the characters we create.

First there are only a tiny amount of primary emotions. Anger, Joy, Fear, and Sadness. These are emotions that are our first reactions to a situation. From there, we move on to secondary emotions. These include greed, pride, envy, love, eagerness, apathy, loneliness, confusion, depression, shame, hate, pride, resentment, and a few more.

Let's now discuss human needs and wants briefly. Abraham Maslow had a theory on human needs that I use in my teaching. The point as to satisfy those needs so that a person could achieve self-actualization. Self-actualization is where one becomes, more or less, "What they should be". In other words, they achieve their full potential or their destiny. Unfortunately, few people ever achieve that level. But from a character standpoint, our heroes normally do. Or they at least make a big step towards it. But to do that, all of the other needs have to be addressed. If not, a person will experience some form of anxiety. Fortunately, there is a rough order to achieving our needs. Here they are:

Level One (Physical needs): breathing, food, water, sleep, bathroom functions, and sex.

Level Two (Safety needs): Security of body, employment, family, health, and property.

Level Three (Love and belonging): Friendship, Family, Intimacy.

Level Four (Esteem): Respect from others, self-esteem, achievement, Respect of others, confidence

Level Five: (Destiny) Self actualization

When you are asked to create a character, you need to develop their backstory. In that backstory, you are fulfilling those needs. Look over each level of needs. List your characters needs and wants by level. Because when one is taken away or not fulfilled, then your character should strive for it. Whatever it is, they are going to want it met. This is their motivation.

The act of combining the emotions and needs together is how we get our characters. If someone has something taken from them, they will get angry. To what level, we don't know. We are not directing them. We are letting them live freely within the moment. This is what Sanford Meisner taught. If a character has all of its level one and two needs met, it will look for friendship, love, and intimacy. What too many people are doing is giving their characters too easy of a life. They aren't making their characters strong, so they fall back on the primary and secondary emotions, rather than the more complex emotions. We are either too lazy to generate the in depth back story our character needs or we are too afraid to make them lacking and vulnerable. I would hope you would overcome your fear of making your character a deep, complex character and instead would give them the attention they deserve. If your group works toward developing strong back stories, your scenes will be significantly much better. You can't make 'em write it though. You certainly can't dictate who their characters are each week. That's just directing. I would challenge you to approach each week's class with vigor. Research your character. Build a strong life for them. Then seek out the stronger actors in class. Because they've put the effort in too. You'll be rewarded emotionally for your efforts. I hear it every week from someone who immersed themselves into their character. They feel alive. They feel like they were that person. That is the entire point of being an actor. To live someone else's life.

Emotions

Affection	Guilt
Anger	Happiness
Annoyance	Hatred
Angst	Hope
Apathy	Horror
Anxiety	Hostility
Awe	Hysteria
Boredom	Jealousy
Compassion	Joy
Contempt	Loathing
Curiosity	Love
Depression	Lust
Desire	Misery
Despair	Pity
Disappointment	Pride
Disgust	Rage
Ecstasy	Regret
Empathy	Remorse
Envy	Sadness
Embarrassment	Shame
Euphoria	Suffering
Fear	Surprise
Frustration	Wonder
Gratitude	Worry
Grief	

The rest of this chapter deals with the back stories of three characters I've created and used in our long form improv scenes at Acting Up! Read through them and find out who they are. Find their strengths and weaknesses. As you develop your characters, use these as foundations in the creation of your characters.

Character 1 - Dr. Meier

From Bellevue Hospital - *I played the hospital doctor in the mental institution. Each student was required to generate a character, including their complete past history. They were required to bring it to me days in advance so that I could study them and "generate" a course of "treatment".*

Dr. K. Lee Meier was born on October 25th, 1925 in the rural town on Pineville, Ky. His parents, John Henry, and Hazel Mardell (nee Groff) were loving, if not unorthodox parents. Raised by a devout Baptist mother, young Meier was frequently in church and even served as a Sunday School teacher in his teens. His father, though officially Baptist, rarely attended. John Henry was known to spout long recitations as to questioning the existence of a God that would allow suffering of so called "faithful servants of God". Meier's paternal grandparents both succumbed to the Spanish Flu epidemic of 1918.

An inquisitive and highly intelligent boy, Meier was accelerated through his primary grades and eventually graduated from Pineville High School in 1942 at the age of 17. Immediately upon graduation, he walked to the recruiting office and enlisted into the U.S. Army Air Forces. Meier's outstanding aptitude scores earned him immediate acceptance into the Officer Candidate School in Miami, FL. He graduated in January 1943 and was assigned to the XIII Bomber Command stationed at Clark Field in Luzon, Philippines. Meier was assigned as the bombardier of a B-17 Flying Fortress. He served on numerous missions in support of the Gilbert and Marshall Islands, the Solomon Islands campaign, and the mission that resulted in the death of Japanese Admiral Yamamoto. He earned two distinguished flying crosses for bravery under fire. His unit was decommissioned in February 1946 at which time he was honorably dismissed from service having attained the rank of Lt. Colonel.

Upon dismissal from military service, he worked for a short time in and around Pineville, Ky. Realizing that a successful career would be unlikely in such a small area, he enrolled at Vanderbilt University in Nashville, TN. While in his freshman year, he enrolled in a basic psychiatry course. Here he met Dr. Petro Tedesco. A strong student-teacher relationship was born that would continue until Dr. Tedesco's death in 1965. Meier earned both his B.S. and M.D. at Vanderbilt. IIis fulfilled his residency requirements in nearby Murfreesboro, TN.

In 1958, Dr. Meier was hired by Bellevue hospital to serve as the initial evaluation psychiatrist. His outstanding work and dedication to his patients has earned him accolades among the mental health community. During the mid 1960s, an influx of Vietnam veterans began to arrive at Bellevue. With no apparent traumatic background to explain their psychosis, Dr. Meier began to investigate whether there was a common thread among the war veterans. Dr. Meier's work along with colleagues, Schnurr, Lunney, and Sengupta has led to the development of a new clinical term, Post-Traumatic Stress Disorder. Dr. Meier continues to evaluate, treat, and improve the lives of war veterans. His work has also expanded to include victims of rape, attempted murder, natural disasters, and other types of physical or psychological trauma.

Character 2 – Buck

From Gunsmoke© – *One of the first long form improv scenes that we have our intermediate students perform is our Old Town Western scene. It is a simple, yet detailed scene set in the local saloon that is run by Buck Dunning. This is always one of my favorite scenes to do.*

John "Buck" Dunning, 41, was born in Montgomery County, Indiana on March 10th, 1831 to William and Jennie Dunning. Buck was the 2nd of 5 children who survived infancy. His younger sister, Georgia, died of tuberculosis at the age of 10. Buck's father was a farmer and shrewd businessman. The family was in no ways rich, but also never fell on hard times. Buck acquired a decent education and studied hard under his father's tutelage. He was a skilled craftsman and by the age of sixteen was selling his furniture at the local general store.

When news broke in 1849 that gold had been discovered in California, Buck immediately took up his possessions and headed west. California was a profitable place for him as he laid claim to a 5 acre plot of prime land that actually produced some gold. In 1853, while Buck was in California, he met a young lady named Esther. They fell in love and were soon engaged. However, for some reason still unknown, Buck took whatever money he had and left California a week before the marriage.

He returned to Indiana and worked on his father's farm until the Civil War broke out. He was called into duty and served with the 86th Indiana Regiment during the war. Never much of a hunter as a young man, he took to the life of a soldier easily and was known for his deadly accurate shooting. During downtimes between battles, the men would sometimes have shooting contests to see who was the best shot. Buck's fellow soldiers soon knew that the only sure fire bet was to place your wager on Buck. Some were so sure he would win, they would wager a whole ten dollars (or "sawbuck") on him, which to a soldier was nearly a half month's wages. It wasn't long and ole "Sawbuck" Dunning was simply known only as Buck.

Buck survived the war intact without a single wound, save a scar on his shin he got from a fall while chasing a rebel soldier while they were on patrol near Huntsville, AL. He did have a scar on his life though, as his father passed from a heart attack in 1864. After the war he headed home to help his mother care for the farm. However, she died of a broken heart in the fall of 1865. In the spring of 1866, Buck left his younger brother to tend the farm as he headed west.

Buck arrived in Dodge City, Kansas on June 8th, 1866. Besides his possessions, he had brought an undisclosed amount of gold with him. He found a local building for sale and after haggling the owner down, made the purchase of what is today Rosie's Cantina. (There has never been anyone own or work there named Rosie. Buck claims he got the name from a song.) Rosie's Cantina is considered one of the best saloons in all of Dodge City and Buck wants to keep it that way. He has very little tolerance for trouble in his establishment. If someone gets too rowdy, he'll call for the sheriff or shoot you, depending on his mood. You can request your favorite drink at Rosie's but you may not get it. Buck has a knack for knowing what drink you really need. And he does not allow any spitting on the floors. There is a two bit fine for anyone caught doing so.

Buck has a business agreement that allows Miss Lilly to run her "business" upstairs from the saloon. He figures it brings in paying customers. He is especially fond of the ladies who work for him and Miss Lilly and won't allow any patrons to bring harm to them. More than one man has left the saloon singing a higher pitch than when he came in. Buck has never married and there are rumors swirling that make people wonder why. Some say he has a mess of gold stashed and doesn't want any woman to get a hold of it. He says he doesn't need a wife. He gets what he wants at work and never has to listen to a woman complain in the morning. Some have suggested he and Miss Lilly marry. Both disagree. They feel they already have a perfect "marriage".

Character 3 – The Big Pasta

*From **The Speakeasy** – In late October each year, it is tradition at Acting Up! to "invite" everyone over to The Cosca to celebrate the birthday of Genoa "The Big Pasta" Rigatoni's birthday. We build a wonderful looking, yet illegal "casino", circa 1925, in the theater. Everyone dresses the part and we have a night of games, food, and fun.*

Genoa "The Big Pasta" Rigatoni, was born on October 25th, 1869 in the little town of Rimini, Italy. The third of 7 children, Genoa was raised a strict Catholic. His parents, Frederico and Isadora, were upper- middle class Italians descended from a long line of hard working families. Genoa was properly educated at the local parochial school. His education included music (piano) and art (oil portraits) in addition to his academic studies. Genoa was considered a highly intelligent boy, but was often caught daydreaming in class. He was highly competitive and it drove him to excel in sports even at an early age. Though not necessarily prone to anger, Genoa was not a fan of losing. It was soon apparent that it was best to be on Genoa's teams. Not only was there a greater chance of winning, but if you did lose, you had no fear of retribution, unless you were the cause of the loss.

In the summer of 1881, his family sold their local business and boarded a steamer to New York. They were processed onto Ellis Island as Italian immigrants on April 15th of that year. Unlike most immigrants, Genoa and his family came to America with money in pocket. They quietly settled into an apartment on the Astoria area of Queens. Frederico found work as a subway construction worker while Isadora raised the seven children. During her spare time, Isadora would sew lovely Italian quilts and sell them to local families. Life was relatively uneventful their first year, but in the early winter of 1882, tuberculosis spread through the tight-knit community. Tragically, Genoa lost his next older brother Felino and his youngest sister Sopressa to the disease.

Genoa secured his first real job in the summer of 1883 when he began to deliver dried goods for the local merchants. Considered an intelligent and hard-working young man, he quickly gained favor with the local businessmen. Genoa wanted to be known as the best delivery boy in Queens and used his competitiveness to his advantage. He found that by pre-planning his daily route and hiring younger boys to assist in his deliveries, he could easily double his daily workload. In no time, Genoa had 6 boys working for him at wages less than he earned from the businessmen he served. This quickly drove the other delivery boys out of business. Within a year, Genoa controlled all the delivery routes of Astoria. On March 15th, 1885, two local thugs ambushed one of his most prominent workers and stole all the goods in addition to badly beating the young man. Two nights later, the same thing happened to another delivery boy. Genoa had to take action. First, he realized he had to vary the delivery routes of his boys. Predictability was a danger to his business. He also hired two large, yet dumb thugs to escort the boys at various times. As the business grew, he hired additional escorts to ensure there no more "unfortunate accidents". By the time he was 16, Genoa had expanded his business beyond his ability to control the day to day planning operations. He knew he needed assistance maintaining the route planning, collecting of money, and the paying of his "hired" help so that he could concentrate on growing his business contacts. So Genoa turned to the person he trusted most, a young lady named Isabella Fiori. They had attended school together since he had arrived in America and he knew her to be not only smart but with the common sense to help him run his business. It didn't hurt that she was also the prettiest girl in the school.

With Isabella's guidance, Genoa's business flourished and it was quickly becoming the largest in all of New York. Genoa knew he needed to make this partnership a lifetime contract so on the evening of December 25th, 1888, as they sat around the fireplace of his parent's home, Genoa asked for her hand in marriage. Not being one to rush into any sort of business arrangement, she made him wait three days before she finally agreed to marry him.

In an extravagant ceremony, the happy couple was married on July 30th, 1889. Never far from each other, the couple has, to this day, held onto that spark that most couples tend to lose. It is well known that should any man (or woman) even think of inappropriately approaching Mrs. Rigatoni, well… let's say it would be the last time they did anything on this planet. The same applies to their one and only child, Antonio. Genoa and Isabella proudly welcomed him into the world on September 2nd, 1892. The Rigatoni's are still waiting for him to marry and give them a grandchild. Hint, hint.. Just sayin'…

Genoa continues to run the largest delivery service in New York. He and Isabella recently returned from a trip to Italy after celebrating 30 years of marital bliss. In spite of his many flaws she still loves him more than anyone. And he knows how lucky he was to find the perfect woman for him.

Mr. and Mrs. Rigatoni would like all their special friends to join them this evening and help them celebrate 30 years of marriage. They have reserved their own special room at The Cosca. Let the celebration begin at 5:30 this evening. Formal attire is required please.

Chapter 10

Motivation and Conflict

"A ship is always safe at the shore but that is not what it is built for"
Albert Einstein

What matters to you? Why does it matter? If someone tries to take something that's important from you, do you stand by and talk about it? Or do you DO something about it? You get emotional about it, don't you? If you aren't getting emotional, then it certainly isn't important to you. It is THE emotional attachment and THE desire to get it back that motivates you.

An actor must make his needs (goals, wants, objectives) so strong that he is willing to interfere with the other actor in order to get what he needs. Interfering means getting in their way so that what you want is stronger than what they want.
Michael Shurtleff

In my school, we stress academics first and foremost to our students. Acting takes a backseat to the fundamentals of our human education. If a student's grades begin to falter, we take the student aside and gently inform that if their grades do not improve, then they will be removed from acting classes until the grades have achieved the level we expect of the student. Normally this is enough motivation to get the student back on track. Sometimes it isn't and we are forced to suspend a student from acting classes for as much as a semester. It isn't something we like to do, but we must always remember what is most important and we hope that this will provide the motivation for the student to improve their academics.

As an actor, we have to look to what our character is trying to achieve. What is the purpose of their journey? Is it to accomplish something? Or are they there to help the protagonist achieve their goal? Is it our character's goal to stop the protagonist? What must be answered is this… What do they NEED to do? What obstacles (conflict) stand in their way? Every character is motivated. As actors, it is our job to dig deep and find that motivation, so that we might overcome the conflict, climb over and beyond the obstacles, and achieve success.

Success requires bravado. It requires risk. As characters and human beings we cannot fear success. We must attack it. As humans we can hide in the background and go through life unfulfilled and eventually die without having achieved the things we were put on this earth to do. But when we create characters, we cannot allow that to happen. We cannot fail as actors. That will only happen if we let them fail in their quests to overcome the obstacles set before them. Our characters certainly do not want to fail. They are motivated to succeed. They are endowed with a purpose. They have been given the skills to realize their dreams. The only thing that can stop them is us.

So how do we ensure our characters are successful? How do we help them prevail over the obstacles that lie before them? We know they are motivated. But we also know they are fallible. Even Superman© had weaknesses. Within a script lie the roots of these weaknesses. The playwright knows them. He wants us to see their weaknesses. And to do so, he creates conflict. He presents us with challenges that we must conquer. Many times, they are small at first, then as the pay progresses, these challenges will become more difficult. But with each obstacle we scale, the strength of our character grows. In time, we are strong enough to fight the ultimate battle. And most times, we will win. Sometimes we fail, but in so doing, we have taught a lesson to others that it is noble to fight the good fight, even when we have faced defeat.

Let's study a very simple, yet effective, example of facing conflict and how motivation can help our characters grow.

The Backstory

Hi, my name is Alan. I'm a 39 year old, not so happily, married man of 17 years. I've got a loving daughter, Allison, and a wife, Julie, who works many late hours. There was a time where my wife and I were very close. Close enough you could call us best friends. But things have changed over the years. She's become very demanding and talking to her is something I try to avoid. I rarely see my wife and when I do she's almost always coming home late and tired from work. To add to it all, I'm stuck in a dead end job and I long for a something to recharge these worn out batteries. I wish things were more like the old days, when life was fun and each day could bring something exciting and new. My daughter gets her license in less than a week and will surely be driving her friends everywhere. So now I am faced with the prospect of sitting at home alone each night, with nothing to ponder except what could be.

I was recently asked to help out at the theater by my best friend Robin. I had called myself a Thespian when I was in college. But that was a long time ago. I was free to do whatever I wanted and I didn't have to answer to anyone. Now things are different. I have work and a daughter. I have obligations. I'm not sure how Julie would feel about me spending my evenings at the theater. She expects me to be home when she arrives. And since she's working so many hours, it's up to me to keep the house presentable.

But I love the theater. And Robin is a great lady and I've known her for many years. She is a beautiful woman with limitless energy. And if she says they need help, then they certainly do. I really had thought about working down there. Maybe even auditioning for a role. Heck, I even helped Robin work through her script. But now I've been given an opportunity. Robin wants me to play the lead opposite her. It's an amazing script. It would be a blast to be on stage again. It would be extra special performing with Robin. But there's a catch. I'd have to kiss her on stage. Yeah, I know we're acting, but what will Julie say? I'm sure she won't like it. Nothing's going to happen between me and Robin. We're great friends, but we're not... well... surely nothing like that would happen, would it?

The Assignment

What does Alan want to do? What is his goal?

What is his motivation to achieve his goal(s)?

_____

_____

_____

_____

_____

_____

What conflict does Alan face? How many obstacles must he overcome?

_____

_____

_____

_____

_____

Resolving Conflict

All stories must eventually come to an end. Unless you're a horror movie franchise which can go on and on. Always remember that we are actors playing a part. This isn't a contest with a winner or loser. Sometimes we're the hero and the audience is rooting for us. Other times we're the bad guy and the audience is hoping to see us fail. In either case, we have to be successful. If we're the bad guy and we have to "fail" in our attempts to defeat the hero, then let's fail epically. There's no reason to leave the audience with a sense of unfulfilled joy from witnessing our demise.

When performing improv we have to strive to reach a conclusion to our story. Sometimes we can achieve it. Other times we won't, but we must be ruthless in our pursuit of closure. To do this we must find a way to resolve the conflict our characters have been sent to overcome. I would like to say that this is an easy thing to achieve, and at times it will be easy to see. Other times it will not. Normally during the course of a scene or set of scenes you will see that plot twist or plot point that makes the conclusion obvious. Always keep in mind that during improvised scenes that there is no set conclusion. As long as you are living in the moment, there will remain numerous possible conclusions. Let me caution you that you should not fight any obvious conclusion to the story arch, even if it means you are the one who must "fail". ** **As characters, we are simply a piece in the overall puzzle of the story and are no more important than any other piece.** ** As I often tell my students, be prepared to fall on your own sword if the story demands that you do so. Your fellow actors and the audience will appreciate your sacrifice.

Chapter 11

Specifics

Always be specific.
Sanford Meisner

Let's start with a little improv game that deals specifically with specifics. We call it "Five Things". You'll need your group of people for this game and an object to pass around. Gather everyone in the circle. One person stands in the center and will be the leader.

To start the game, hand the object to any person. For our purposes, let's say we're using a Styrofoam cup and we'll have you be the leader. When you say "go", the person will pass the cup to their right. Using the list below (or your own list), you will then say for example "5 types of birds". The first person has to give you five types of birds before the cup makes its way around the circle back to the person who started. If they do not give the five things, then they're out of the game. If they do come up with five items, then the cup stops when the last of the five items is called out. The person holding the cup is now the starter and you will give them a different idea to generate five items from.

This game teaches not only specifics, but also exercises the brain and teaches it to think faster. If your group is small or as players are eliminated, you can have each person come up with only three items. This is a very enjoyable game to play.

Five Things

1. Types of dogs
2. Types of fish
3. Continents
4. Famous people
5. Inventions
6. Books of the Bible
7. Religions
8. Farm animals
9. Countries in Europe
10. Famous movie actors
11. Types of insects
12. Horror movies
13. Professions
14. Professional sports
15. Movie characters
16. Songs
17. States that start with "I"
18. Pieces of clothing
19. Pasta dishes
20. Flavors of Kool-Aid
21. Dead presidents
22. Improv games
23. Branches of the military
24. Weapons you can kill with
25. Types of salad dressings
26. Electronic devices
27. Video games
28. Types of meat
29. Condiments
30. Colors of crayons not red or blue
31. Cartoon characters
32. Serial killers
33. Musical groups
34. Reality TV shows
35. Brands of shoes

Did you have fun? Add to this list and see how many obscure ideas you can come up with. The greater your diversity of ideas, the more the mind is exercised. Just like physical exercise stimulates the muscles to grow, mental exercise stimulates the brain and helps generate more synapses. And we can all stand to use our brains a little more!

There are many things we can talk about when dealing with specifics. When I use that term, I mean, literally, all the details that make a character, a set, the reasons for the conflict, and on and on. You as an actor have several things that you must answer. And you need to be specific about the specifics.

First, you need to know the specifics of your character. Who are you? What are you doing or supposed to do? Where are you or where are you going? When is this happening? And finally why are you doing all that your character needs to do?

In chapter 10, you're going to answer all those questions. Your job at this point is to gather your information. Create a list. Don't cut this part short. The more you understand the specifics, the better prepared you will be to deliver a quality performance.

In preparing for a role, it is also encouraged and sometimes demanded that you know the time period and as much about the location as you possibly can. Here is a sample worksheet my students used to help them prepare for a 1920s Speakeasy scene. Use this worksheet to do your own research. Note - There will be a quiz at the end.

1. What is a speakeasy?

_____

_____

_____

_____

_____

_____

2. During what time period did they reach their peak?

_____

3. What was Prohibition?

_____

_____

_____

_____

_____

4. What type music was popular during the time? Name two musicians of the time.

_____

_____

5. What type of dance was popular during the time? Name two dances of the time.

_____

_____   _____

6. What style of clothing did the women and men wear?

_____

_____

7. Name three famous gangsters/bootleggers of the time.

_____

_____

_____

8. Name 3 illegal activities often found in a speakeasy.

_____

_____

_____

9. ** Bonus Points ** What does the name "Cosca" mean?

_____

_____

_____

Chapter 12

Auditioning

Simply put, having a successful audition is all about having **ATTITUDE!** But let me caution you. You need to be a professional at all times. You cannot win casting directors, producers, directors, etc. over with smiles and charisma. They are important, but they've seen it thousands of times. You'll win them over much quicker with a professional attitude.

Generally auditions are conducted in the casting director's office, the theatre or even the studio. Be polite to everyone, including the assistant at the desk outside the office. When you enter the auditioning room, acknowledge everyone. Be courteous, smile, and maintain a professional air about you. And stayed focused on why you are there. Now it's time to prepare to do what you do best. Give them your very best work.

Come to the audition as if you are at a job interview. Wear appropriate but not too fancy clothes. Khakis and a nice shirt for the men. A simple suit or dress slacks for the ladies.

Have your 8" x 10" headshot ready for them when you arrive. Either attach your resumé to the back, or have it printed directly to the back of your 8" x 10".

You should expect to sign in when you get there. It can be a nightmare to keep everyone organized otherwise, so once you arrive, seek out where to sign in. Provide all the information they are asking for including, but not limited to your union affiliation, such as the Screen Actors Guild (SAG).

Many times when I conduct auditions, I will videotape them. So be aware that you could be videotaped. If you are don't worry. You could be asked to "slate." All that means, is that you should look into the camera lens, state your name, any role you may be auditioning for, and the agency that represents you, if you are represented. After that, it's time to audition.

First things first. Don't ever panic. We're all humans and we make mistakes. If you lose your place in the script or you lose concentration for a moment, pause and ask to restart the audition. Or if you would like to show another interpretation, ask if you can. There is no guarantee they'll let you restart or do another version, but normally they will. If they don't give you a second chance, then thank them politely for the opportunity and wish them luck on their project. And then leave the room.

If this is an audition where you will be performing a prepared monologue you will be expected to know your lines completely. You will have two, perhaps three minutes with which to complete your audition for the director or casting agent. You may be asked to do a cold read. If so, use what little time you have wisely. Prepare the material the best you can and deliver it with conviction. DO NOT use the preparation time to talk with other actors. Remember, they're there to take your job away from you!

Ultimately, the only thing that matters is your performance. Give it your best, but when it's over, it's over. Don't go home and fret about it. Live in the Moment!!! What's done is done. If you can learn from anything you did or didn't do, then use it to improve for the next time. Otherwise, put that audition aside and begin preparing for the next one.

There are a lot more actors out there than there are parts. Being turned down is part of the business. It might not have been your performance, so don't take it personally. I have turned down numerous actors and actresses not for their audition, but simply because they didn't fit the "look" of the role. Likewise, I've cast people in roles that originally they didn't fit into, but because they were so good I had to find a place for them. Sometimes that included a rewrite of the script.

Chapter 13

I GOT THE ROLE!!!

Congratulations. Now sit down and be quiet. No one wants you rubbing it in. We all auditioned for a part. A lot of us didn't make it, you know.

That's right. Be happy you got the role. Be excited. But don't rub it in others people's faces. Who knows, maybe you'll need to work with them on stage someday. Maybe someday they'll be a director. Best not to tick anyone off early in your career.

Now you've got some work to do. You should be hearing from the director or their staff very soon. They will get you a script. They should get you a rehearsal or shooting schedule soon too. They may need to schedule a costume fitting. They may call you. They may email you. Or send it via regular postal mail. In any case, always, and I repeat, always be courteous. Say "Yes, sir" or "Yes, ma'am". They are now your boss. Don't think for an instant that just because you got the lead that you're now in charge. We'll knock you off that pedestal real quick. The director is the artistic vision. Remember Rule #4? The director is ALWAYS right. You may suggest changes or ask the director to see your interpretation of a part of the script, but you must always let them have the final say. Do not argue with the director or their assistants. Be professional at all times. No one likes a drama queen. Or king!

Once you get the script, read it from front to back. Know the complete story, even if your role doesn't have any lines. If you have lines, then start memorizing them. We've been over how to approach the script. Make every effort to walk into the first rehearsal with your lines memorized. It makes everyone else's job must easier. Don't worry if you're unsure how the lines are to be delivered. That's the director's job. They'll guide you through it. It's very possible they will want to see your interpretation of the character. That's fine too. Do your best to show them how you see the character. Then listen to the director and make the adjustments they ask for. Perhaps they'll ask for a change in emphasis in the way the lines are delivered. Or perhaps they'll ask you to add a little accent. Don't panic if you don't get it right immediately. You tell the director that you're going to go home and work hard on it before the next rehearsal.

Rehearsals can be become very tiring and tedious, especially if you're prepared and others aren't. Do your best to hide your frustration. Let the director deal with the less prepared actors. You're there to do a job. To do it well. And to do it with enthusiasm. The director, set designers, costumers, and every other person involved with the production is under tremendous pressure. Don't add to it by being late to rehearsals or by being demanding. Walk in ready to work and with a smile on your face. You're an actor BECAUSE YOU WANT TO BE. No one forces you to be an actor.

It may seem like you have plenty of time before the show opens. Trust me, those last few weeks will fly by. The frenzy of activity at the theater will grow exponentially in anticipation of dress rehearsal, tech rehearsal, and finally the performance(s). Things rarely run smoothly during dress and/or tech rehearsal. Don't worry about it. Whenever I've been a director, I almost preferred that there actually BE problems during those rehearsals. It reminded us that we needed to maintain our focus on all the details. A flawless rehearsal scares me to death, because I fear people will become too relaxed and complacent. Don't be that person.

If you've never performed on stage or performed in a play that required a technical (tech) rehearsal, let me tell you briefly how they work. This rehearsal is for the technical crew. They tend to run substantially longer than a dress rehearsal. The crew is going to set the final lighting. They're going to work on special effects, if necessary. They are going to make sure all set pieces are ready and that all set changes happen quickly and flawlessly. There are going to be sound and music checks. You may be asked to do certain scenes over and over to get the technical aspects dialed in. You may be asked to stand in one spot for a period of time so that they can adjust the spot or flood lights. They may try different colored gels on the lights that will compliment or enhance your makeup or costume. Be patient during this time. All of these technical elements are there to make the performance great.

The week leading up to the performances normally consist of the dress rehearsal, tech rehearsal, and what will seem like endless additional rehearsals in preparation of opening night. You WILL be busy. You WILL have long nights. You WILL be tired. Don't get frustrated. All the hard work is about to pay off. When those lights come up on the stage for opening night, you will experience one of the greatest feelings of your life. Few things compare to performing on stage. Don't let your nerves get to you. Take some deep breaths and try to relax. Drink plenty of water in the week leading up to the performance. You do not want to become dehydrated. Take care of your body AND your mind. Don't stay out any later than you have to.

Get plenty of sleep. You certainly don't want to wear yourself out and end up sick.

Speaking of ending up sick, what happens if you do? Normally, larger plays have understudies. But what happens if you are in one that doesn't? Well, that of course, depends on how sick you are. Unless you simply cannot perform, find a way, anyway, to get out there on stage. I was in that situation a few years ago. I had a very substantial role in a play and had no understudy. And my part included two high energy dances. Our technical rehearsal was the day before the play and I woke up that morning sick with a fever. I called the director and told her of my condition. I was supposed to be there at 10:00 a.m., but she told me to take some aspirin and rest and that we would push the technical rehearsal back to noon in hopes that the fever would break by then. It did. For a short period of time. I made it to the theater and we began rehearsing. Remember me telling you how long technical rehearsals can run? This one ran for almost 5 hours! When I walked off the stage, my fever had hit 103 degrees and my body in a bad way. All I could do was take some meds and lie down because we had dress rehearsal at 7:00 that night!

I made it through dress rehearsal somehow and then through the night. But when I awoke the next morning I was still sick. Very sick. And we had two performances that day. I took every bit of medication I could think of that might make me feel better. I drank fluids galore. I rested every moment I could. (I found a hospital bed backstage and took up residence on it.) Fortunately for me, I had a team of nurses trying to get me well. Our play included a lot of young children and ten girls (literally) were taking turns running to the bathroom to get cool rags for my head. They were bringing me drinks. I felt like a king on his throne. Well, their work paid off. 30 minutes before the first performance, my fever broke. Though I was still tired and a bit weak, I was able to get through the performance. No way was I going to let down all the people who helped me and all those who had worked on the play. Between performances the fever returned and that same team of little nurses worked their magic, but this time the fever broke 45 minutes before the performance. Two days later I was at the doctor being treated for strep throat. (No one contracted it other than me.)

To this day, I know we were a little lucky. My illness could have been disastrous. I also know we had a lot of people believing in us. And I had ten little angels who were not going to let anything happen to me or the play. So the next time you're not feeling well, remember that the show MUST GO ON. You would be surprised what magic the theater can work, when you allow it to.

Chapter 14

Handling the Script

The words within a script are irrelevant. They are nothing more than chatter projected by actors to an audience. Whoa! Stop right there! What do you mean that the words don't mean anything? Isn't the play filled with words? Sure it is, but by themselves they mean nothing. I can recite all the words in the play and it will have zero impact on you. But as an actor I have a chance to breathe life into the words. It's what we do with the words that count. It's how we treat them. It's how we nurture them and help them grow.

Acting doesn't have anything to do with listening to the words. We never really listen, in general conversation, to what the other person is saying. We listen to what they mean. And what they mean is often quite apart from the words. When you see a scene between two actors that goes really well you can be sure they're not listening to each other -- they're feeling what the other person is trying to get at. Know what I mean?

Jack Lemmon

When first handed a script, resist the desire to read it immediately. Yes, I want you to wait. Don't skim through it in the theater. I want you to wait until your mind is clear and there are no distractions around you. I want you to find a quiet place to read it. I want your mind free to see the words. If you have access to a script you've never read, go get it. There are several good, free ones on the internet. I'll just sit here while you go get it…

Still waiting….

Haven't gone anywhere…

Any time now…

Got it? Yes? No? Don't have one? Lucky for you I've included one for us to work with.

Before we get to the script though, I want to make a couple things clear. When you read this, I want you to resist reading it with your interpretation of how it should be "performed". I want you just read the words. Let them talk to you. For the time being, they are your scene partner. Listen to them. Let them speak to you. But DO NOT READ THEM ALOUD!

Summer and Winters by Kevin L. Meier

BILLY and PAUL, two eighteen year old boys, are standing by the creek throwing and skipping rocks.

BILLY: Do you realize how lucky we are?

PAUL: How lucky are we?

BILLY: We graduate in just one month. And we're getting to go to college. On scholarships!

Billy bends over to pick up another rock.

PAUL: (Not listening to Billy.) I'm going to go to Paris, Billy.

Billy stops throwing rocks and turns toward Paul.

BILLY: You're what?

PAUL: I'm going to Paris for the summer. I've decided I can't stay here and risk seeing Darlene with Alex anymore. I think I need some time away.

BILLY: Wait! Did you say, Paris? As in Paris, Illinois?

PAUL: No! Paris, France, you idiot. I told you I was going to do it one day.

BILLY: If you need time away, then go to Indianapolis.

PAUL: I'm going to Paris. I'm gonna spend my summer there.

BILLY: The whole summer? What about our plans?

PAUL: I know. I'm sorry. I just can't be around here, now. I can't be around her.

BILLY: (Disappointed.) Yeah, I guess. What kind of jerk comes in and steals his best friend's girl?

PAUL: I wish I knew.

BILLY: Well, I hope he loses all his hair and Darlene gets big and fat and her tits fall to the floor.

Billy walks around trying to hold up huge, imaginary breasts.

PAUL: (Laughing.) Stop it! That's not a site I want to have burned into my brain. (Gets serious.) Really though, I hope she's happy. I hope this is what she wants.

BILLY: How can you say that? They ran around behind your back for nearly a year.

PAUL: Yeah, I just wish she would have told me.

BILLY: That would have been a whole lot easier than catching them behind Ole Johnson's barn.

PAUL: You're telling me.

BILLY: Might have saved Alex a broken nose.

PAUL: (Smiling.) I think the blood ruined his shirt.

BILLY: Serves him right.

An awkward pause as the boys reflect.

PAUL: Do you remember the stories Mrs. Babineaux used to tell us about France?

BILLY: Of course. She made it sound like a little piece of heaven.

PAUL: That's why I'm going, because I've been through hell here.

BILLY: So you think a summer in Paris is gonna help you get over her.

PAUL: I don't know, but I have to get away. I need a change of scenery. I'd like to find a little cafe and just watch the people. I want to see what Mrs. Babineaux used to tell us about. I want to see the Eiffel Tower and the Louvre. I want to walk down the Champ Elysees and sit in that little café and drink French wine. I have to get out of Indiana, Billy. I have to get away from Darlene and Alex.

BILLY: But you'll be back for the start of school?

PAUL: Of course. It's just one summer.

Now put the script away. Go think about what you read and come back tomorrow.

Back already? Sleep well? Good. We read the script yesterday, so we're familiar with the story. Since we've come into the middle of a story, there isn't a lot of information told about the characters Billy and Paul. Before we begin with the next part of our exercise I want you to take a few minutes and tell us a little bit about each character. Don't forget to include the conflict and motivation for each character.

BILLY

_____

_____

_____

_____

_____

_____

_____

PAUL

_____

_____

_____

_____

_____

_____

_____

Well done. Now I want you to grab a piece of paper and a pen. Or for the penmanship challenged, you can use a computer. I want you to write this scene out in its entirety, but without any of the playwright's notes or any punctuation. The reason I have you do this is two-fold. One it will help you learn the lines, but it will also take you away from how you feel the playwright wants you to perform this piece. There are many ways to perform a scene. What he has written is only one. To truly live in the moment, you must be ready to perform this scene in more than one way.

Now that we've removed the elements that control how the scene was written to be performed, it's time to start working on the lines. But all I want you to do is read the script as it is with no punctuation. Do not add any emphasis to the lines at this time. Simply begin to memorize the lines.

Now is the time to find a scene partner. Make sure they are as prepared as you are. Once they are, we're going to do our first read together, so find a table and go sit down. I will caution you here to not add the emotion you think the director will want to see. Do not add any actions or movements that you think your scene partner expects. We are living in the moment, right? If you walk in and perform the scene as you think it should be done, you will do it marginally good at best, and will most likely never discover the real potential that lies in your character and in this play.

The key to this first read is to simply work on the script word by word, syllable by syllable. Digest the words. Sound them out slowly and clearly. Don't read them in a way that makes you sound like a robot, but let them flow easily, like a nice stream of water. Don't worry about looking at your scene partner as you read them. This is about listening to the words. Maybe this exercise is a bit confusing to you, but trust me, it isn't as hard as it may sound. Once you begin, it'll be quite evident what you're doing. For full length plays, this can take a long time to go completely through the script. That's fine. With any script, if time permits, repeat this exercise.

Now it's time to move on. Get everyone back together and we're going to do the "working read". Just like before, we're going to sit down at the table and go through our lines. But this time we're going to bring emphasis to the lines. As you go through the script, take in as many words as you can, look up at your scene partner and recite them. They don't have to be the exact words. Getting it close is perfectly fine. We're not just listening here. We're also talking. Talking as if this is a real conversation. Remember to live in the moment. At this point you'll begin to work and play off each other. Do not do anything to stifle any spontaneous moments. Let them happen naturally.

It's not uncommon for my actors to sit down and discuss the play at this point. This is the time they begin seeking information about the other characters and how the actor is going to play them. There is a tremendous amount of back stories told. They talk of how their character reached this point in their life and where they see them going. It's also perfectly acceptable to have the "characters" sit down and tell everyone about themselves. There is nothing wrong with getting into character for a little impromptu discussion.

So are you ready to start memorizing? I'd say you've probably already started getting a handle on the script by this point. You've been through it several times and the story line is familiar to you. Now is when I want you to start memorizing the lines. What I don't want you to memorize, though, is the emotions. I don't want you locked in to a set way of performing this piece. I want you to be able to be free enough that you can explore the many ways a piece can be interpreted.

Memorizing lines is a very personal thing and each individual is different, so I don't want to say that one way works better than any other. Some people I know write down every line. Others memorize it scene by scene. Personally, I memorized my lines in sequence. I would learn a line, then cover it up and after having read the line before mine, try to recite my line. If I got it correct, I moved to the next. After each line was memorized, I would recite all I had learned in order. This works for me. It may or may not work for you.

I cannot stress enough how important it is to COMPLETELY memorize your lines. Not 99% correct. Not 99.9% correct. You MUST have them down to the point that that you do not need to think about them when the time comes to say them. If you have to think about your next line, you are taking away your ability to properly listen and react to what is happening on stage. You must make the lines as automatic as you possibly can. This will free you to improvise, react, and live freely in the moment during a performance.

Theater Terms and Definitions

The best place to start here would be with a layout of the stage and the term "blocking". Blocking is defined as "defining the basic movements of and actor during a play". But to understand what the director wants you to do and where they want you to go, you need to understand the terms of the stage. See the diagram below for reference:

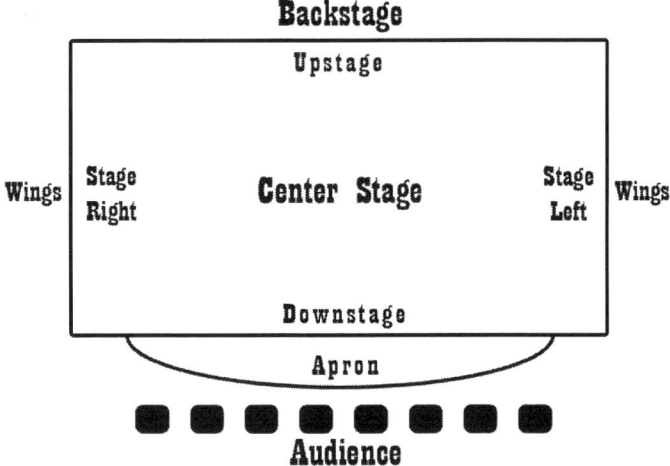

The stage is laid out from the point of reference of the actor. Stand center stage and face the audience. If the director tells you to go "stage right", move to your right toward the wings. If the director tells you to now go "upstage left", then go to the back of the stage and to the left wings. It's that simple. Now you may ask why "upstage" is back and "downstage" is forward. In the olden days of theater, the stage used to be sloped so that actors in the back of the stage could be seen over the actors at the front of the stage. Stages are now normally flat, but the terminology remains.

The remainder of this chapter will deal with a few specific terms that I think you will find useful in your studies as an actor. This is far from being all inclusive.

Act: A major division of a play. Usually divided into scenes.

Antagonist: The character who provides conflict for the protagonist and presents the obstacle for the protagonist to overcome.

Apron: The area of the stage in front of the curtain.

Backdrop: A set piece, normally made of canvas, that has been painted to represent the setting of the play. Normally hung from the flies at the back of the stage.

Call back: The second stage of the audition process for those who are under serious consideration for a part.

Cheat: To turn the body out toward the audience while talking to another character.

Cross: A stage direction that has the actor move from one side of the stage to the other.

Flies: The area above the stage, hidden from the audience, to which backdrops are attached.

Hit your mark: A stage direction for an actor to hit a certain "mark" on the stage and deliver a line or to make an entrance on cue.

Mark: Literally a mark on the stage for an actor to be at when delivering a particular line.

Off book: When an actor has all of his or her lines memorized.

Pace: The speed at which a play is performed.

Protagonist: The lead character and hero of the story.

Run lines: To recite the lines of the play without the blocking.

Thalia and Melpomene: The Greek masks of comedy and tragedy.

Thespis: Greek Poet (550-500 B.C.) who is considered the founding father of dramatic theater. From which we get thespian.

Understudy: Actor who is prepared to take over an important role should the main actor be unable to perform.

Voice projection: The control and volume of an actor's voice so that even those in the last role can hear and understand all the dialogue of a play.

Chapter 16

After the Curtain Falls

We stood at the edge of the stage holding hands. The curtain having already fallen for the final time. And in it laid the painfully symbolic reality of the moment. Neither of us talked. We only stood there. Lost in the silence. Lost in the moment. Knowing that years of working together were coming to an end. No more teacher/student. She was now an adult. About to leave and venture out into the world on her own. All I could hope for was that I had taught her well. Emotions, projection, living in the moment. Living in this moment. Not wanting it to end. Yes, I would see her on Broadway and in Hollywood movies, but what I wouldn't see is her. Not in this way ever again. How I would miss her. Her smile. Her laughter. The fire that burned within her. She had become one of my closest friends through these 8 years together. All the times we had talked. The times we had played. The performances and rehearsals. The blood and sweat of bringing life to the stage. All the laughter and fun we had shared. All the hard work and even the tears. Then, as if reading my mind, she turned to me. I saw a single tear falling slowly down her cheek. The pain filled her eyes. She was telling me how much she loved me. How much I had done for her. And then I was crying, because I loved her like a daughter. But we had a bond that went beyond that. Something that would keep our hearts together forever. We stood there. Holding hands. Searching for words that would never come. And then she pulled herself close and kissed me so gently upon my cheek. Then, without a word, she turned and walked away. I watched her walk up the aisle, knowing that her heart was breaking and knowing that this time there was nothing I could do. As she reached the door, she paused. Turning, she looked to me. "I will always love you", she said. Then, she turned and walked out the door. There, once again, I stood alone as a single tear fell upon the silent stage.

The story is fictitious. The emotions are not. Because I teach primarily teenagers and pre-teens, the inevitable fact remains. They will graduate and move on. If I dwelled on them leaving, I could easily become very depressed. We are a close knit family and watching one of my "children" grow up and move on is never easy. But to get through it, I have to treat it as if it is just one chapter in a book or one scene of a larger play, be it a very special one.

And so goes the plays that you will perform in. When I was young and only performing in one or two plays a year, I found that closing night was a very sad time for me. I was proud of the work I had done, but I was sad that the time with my friends, teachers, and directors was over. I didn't know it at the time, but down deep I was sad that my time with and as my character was over. Now when I play a role, I relish the time I have as my character. I grab it and run with it and I refuse to let go until the final curtain falls. I don't want to walk away and say "what if I had done this or done that". I want to know that I gave my all. Then I know I can walk away with a smile on my face because I brought the character to life. I gave him a personality. More importantly, I gave him a soul.

Chapter 17

The Code of Honor

We are "professional" actors, regardless of whether we are paid to perform or not. I tell all my students to work, perform, and live the life as if you were a professional. We never know what may happen in our lives. Perhaps a commercial opportunity arrives. Or some unknown director may be sitting in the audience some night hoping to find that one special talent. Accordingly, we hold ourselves to the highest standards as actors and as human beings. For students who earn the right to be enrolled in any of our professional classes or for those even luckier few who are part of our traveling improv troupe, The Nuclear ReActors, they are all required to sign our Code of Honor. This is their reminder that for all the work they've done to this point, the real work now lies ahead. They are now ambassadors of our school. They are role models to the younger (and sometimes older) students. We do not take this responsibility lightly, but instead embrace it wholeheartedly. In essence, in all that we do. We live it. We breathe it. We believe it!

(Many thanks to Patti Hutchison, Tom Fulton and Kathleen Freeman for their inspiration in forming this Code of Honor.)

Code of Honor

I will embrace a life-long study of my art as a performer as long as my heart aspires to do so.

I promise to care and nurture my body, voice, mind, feelings and spirit, which are the instruments of my art. I will not do things that will knowingly harm me or my spirit.

I am neither superior nor inferior to others and will treat everyone as an equal. We are each individuals.

I will not discriminate against anyone regardless of race, gender, religion, class, sexual orientation, or disability.

I will make everyone feel as if they belong. We are a family.

I will make everyone feel safe from bodily or psychological harm or humiliation. I will ensure they are able to speak freely without fear of retribution.

I will make my scene partner look good. I will give each and all of my fellow performers my full and undivided attention and preserve an atmosphere of creativity for all.

I promise to open up my mind so that I might imagine great things without reserve or fear. I will give everyone the chance to express themselves without fear of being judged.

I will encourage all my fellow performers. I will be generous with praise for their hard work. I will welcome new performers and welcome the opportunity to learn from them.

I will lead by example, giving freely of my knowledge and experiences so that others can advance from my work.

I am responsible for my actions. I will make a conscious effort to realize my actions affect others. If I fail, I will admit it and commit to changing my faulty behavior.

I will also strive to respect my instincts and follow my impulses, without judgment or self doubt. For the energy of life is found when we live within the moment.

As the theater is the home of my heart, I will work to respect her and always wipe my feet at the door, leaving it a cleaner and safer place than when I arrived.

I will approach my work in the theater with gratitude, regardless of how or if I am cast. It is a privilege to be allowed the opportunity to create life upon the stage.

I will accept my artistic struggles and failures without self-doubt. Success is built upon the determination and courage to overcome one's obstacles and become the person you were meant to be.

I will receive and accept other's criticism without bitterness, because I realize they have seen me with eyes that are not my own.

I will respect my teachers, fellow actors, and mentors for it is through them that priceless knowledge can be found. I shall always strive, be it in rehearsal or performance, so that I might work in harmony and with the high standards they have set before me.

I shall never miss a performance.

I understand the importance of rehearsing my art. I will use my gifts faithfully, and through practice, attain a higher knowledge of my talents and my fellow players' talents.

I shall play every performance with energy, enthusiasm and to the best of my ability regardless of size of audience, personal illness, bad weather, or accident.

I shall forego all social activities which interfere with rehearsals or any other scheduled work at the theatre, and I shall always be on time.

I shall forego the gratification of my ego for the demands of the play.

I shall never "put on an act" while viewing other artists' work as a member of an audience, nor shall I make caustic criticism from jealousy or for the sake of being smart.

I shall respect the play and the playwright and, remembering that "a work of art is not a work of art until it is finished," I shall not condemn a play while it is in rehearsal.

I shall not spread rumor or gossip which is malicious and tends to reflect discredit on my show, the theatre, or any personnel connected with them - either to people inside or outside the group.

I shall accept my director's and producer's direction and guidance in the spirit in which it is given, for they see the production as a whole.

I shall remember my business is to suspend disbelief and thus create illusion; therefore, I shall not break the illusion by appearing in costume and makeup off-stage or outside the theatre.

I will continually strive to "love the art in myself, and not myself in the art."

I understand that membership as a Thespian entitles me to the privilege of working, when I am so assigned, in any of the phases of a production, including: props, lights, sound, construction, house management, box office, publicity and stage managing-as well as acting. I realize it is possible I may not be cast in a part for many months, but I will not allow this to dampen my enthusiasm or desire to work, since I realize without my willingness to do all other phases of theatre work, there would be no theatre for me to act in.

With this vow, I dedicate myself to theatre as an art and will celebrate these promises as I study, as I rehearse, and as I play.

Might I challenge you to take this vow?

You can sign your name right here

_____

Chapter 18

Scene Starters

One of the greatest challenges I face, is to come up with new scenes each week. My students quickly tire of me getting them "lost in the woods" or "stranded in a lifeboat". So I've included many of the scene starters we have used through the years. Feel free to modify them in any way you need to help generate your scene. Try to use them in different games to get different variations of scene results.

Opening lines

This is to teach reaction. Use them in the following manner. One person should step on stage. The second person selects one of the opening lines listed below, steps on stage and says the exact line with no additional dialogue until their scene partner reacts. Use all the emotion the line requires, but don't add to it. Your scene partner should have no idea what you're about to say. This allows them to live freely in the moment and react genuinely to your opening line.

1. I need you in my life.
2. I hate you!
3. Let's spend the night together.
4. I have terminal cancer.
5. I'm afraid.
6. I had a lot of fun tonight.
7. It's weird how we've become best friends.
8. Memorize your lines!
9. People think we're, you know... they're talking about us.
10. I'm so in love with you.
11. The ambulance is on the way.

12. Don't volunteer for any suicide missions.
13. I'm pregnant.
14. Please, just once.
15. I saw you kiss her.
16. They repossessed the car.
17. Just do as you're told!
18. If you're gonna do it, do it.
19. Touch me like you used to do.
20. Please don't hurt me.
21. The bank is taking our home
22. Stop being a jerk!
23. Stop joking around.
24. You're a coward.
25. This isn't the way it's supposed to be.
26. Leave her or else.
27. (Without a word, walk in and kiss the person.)
28. (Without a word, break down crying.)
29. (Without a word or touch, show them how much you love them.)
30. (Without a word, show them how mad you are.)
31. (Without a word, break down crying.)
32. (Without a word or touch, show them how much you desire them.)
33. That was my sister!
34. Life isn't all about jokes.
35. I wish I had been there for you.
36. This is your child.
37. I hate life and I hate you!
38. We won't last.
39. I need you to help me kill my parents.
40. You're gonna pay for this.
41. The sooner you die, the better.
42. Show some compassion.
43. We could make beautiful music together.
44. Let's give them something to talk about!
45. I thought we had something special.
46. You're a pathetic piece of …

47. If I leave tomorrow will you still remember me?
48. Come on, let's just go and never look back.
49. Oh yes it is a brilliant idea.
50. What are you afraid of?
51. So what if it happens?
52. It's not going to kill you.
53. Put that down and help!
54. Yeah, it's my fault.
55. I wish I would have known that was going to happen.
56. Are you a ghost?
57. I don't think we're in Kansas anymore.
58. This looks like the perfect place to set up camp.
59. I saw you naked.
60. I have a plan.
61. I was a spy stationed in Istanbul, Turkey.
62. Welcome to hell.
63. I have a fear of clowns and midgets.
64. I really don't care.
65. Life isn't much fun right now.
66. That's the dumbest idea I've heard all day.
67. Probably best if you just help with the set or something.
68. I'll never forgive myself for what I did to you.
69. Have you seen any spare clothes around here?
70. She's right behind you.
71. Stop making excuses and go for it.
72. Stop whining!
73. Tie her down.
74. I know something about Philip.
75. Which way to the boat?
76. One of us isn't coming back.
77. What were you thinking?
78. Why did you bring *IT* with you?
79. Guys, we're lost.
80. Truth or dare?
81. Cut, cut, cut!
82. We're out of food and water.
83. If you leave me now.

84. Everything I do, I do it for you.
85. You are so beautiful to me.
86. I will be waiting.
87. You're as stiff as a frozen deer carcass.
88. I often pray before I lay down.
89. We should cherish the life we have.
90. If only you could read my mind.
91. Heroes often fail.
92. I don't know where we went wrong.
93. I don't know where the feelings went, but I can't get them back.
94. I'd really love to see you tonight.
95. I was thinking maybe later on we could get together.
96. I'm not asking for promises so you don't have to lie.
97. Just once.
98. What are we doing wrong?
99. Baby, you're the best.
100. There were people runnin' everywhere.
101. Don't bother knocking on my door this time.
102. Think about it, there must be a greater love.
103. Look inside your heart and I'll look inside mine.
104. I can't go on wondering if you'll be here tomorrow.
105. There's a line that I can't cross over.
106. They'll never take away what we have.
107. Someone stranger saved my life tonight.
108. You almost had your hooks in me.
109. You're like a butterfly, free to fly.
110. I'm sure I can be a movie star.
111. It's a pretty good crowd for a Friday night.
112. Sometimes I think it's a shame.
113. The ending's too hard to take.
114. Let's be real.
115. I never thought I could act this way.
116. I don't know where we went wrong.
117. I never thought I could feel this way.
118. And a wave broke over the railing.
119. Then where am I to go?

120. I found her diary.
130. You gave my life back to me.
131. She taught me how to love.
132. I know it's kinda late.
133. I would all I own if you would just come back to me.
134. Yeah, I know it's strange.
135. There never seems to be enough time for us.
136. Isn't that the way they say it goes?
137. I finally understand what you tried to say to me.
138. Did you write the book of love?
139. I know you're in love with him.
140. But we never even got a chance!
141. I love you, too.
142. It was the heat of the moment.
143. I ain't got no crystal ball.
144. It's good to be back home.
145. The sweetest thing is just spending time with you.
146. I want to watch you die.
147. Does it worry you to be all alone?
148. Do you believe in love at first sight?
149. Don't fear death.
150. And then the firemen rush in.
151. And I won't think about sticking that gun straight down his throat.
152. How could we be so blind?
153. Someday, love will find you.
154. You know I still love you.
155. I don't know where I'll be tomorrow.
156. Well I just heard the news.
157. I don't know if I'm ready.
158. We've seen our share of ups and downs.
159. I don't want this night to end.
160. There are two paths you can choose.
161. You think that something's happening?
162. Tell me if it's wrong or right?
163. I gave, now I'm wanting something in return.
164. You have made me who I am.

165. I don't understand why you don't treat yourself better.
166. Did you do it out of love?
167. This is just what I needed.
168. At least you could try and act like you belong here.
169. You didn't deserve to win.
170. You been telling your friends you gonna be a star.
171. I need a woman that's gonna make me a happy man.
172. I feel like a change is gonna do me some good.
173. This ain't how it's supposed to be.
174. I am passionate!
175. Yes, I used to be in love with you.
176. I've been waiting for this moment my whole life.
177. This place looks familiar, but I've never been here.
178. So what if I did it?
179. Things aren't what they appear to be.
180. Big risk equals big reward.
181. You are a traitor!
182. This is the way nightmares begin.
183. I kissed you in a dream last night.
184. Thanks for the times that you've given me.
185. I tried to make you happy.
186. We each made our own mistakes.
187. There's no other love.
188. Don't be afraid.
189. You don't have to ask twice.
190. I can't live without you.
191. If there ever comes a day where you need to walk away, I'll understand.
192. I'm not kidding around.
193. Just once, please.
194. You gotta break free.
195. I am in charge of my destiny.
195. Love doesn't exist.
196. I'm going to kiss you.
197. Take one step closer and I'll smack you.
198. You don't understand me.
199. It's all true.

200. I would never lie to you about this.
201. You can do it.
202. My dad thinks you're hot.
203. All you are is a shooting star, that's falling fast.
204. I'm gonna make the big time.
205. I guess he OD'd on pain killers.
206. I have no pity for you.
207. You brought this on yourself.
208. Let's just go and never look back.
209. Let's dance in the rain.
210. It's my life!
211. I thought he was a chick!
212. You just won an academy award!
213. I don't have a good feeling about this.
214. Haven't we met before?
215. I know you won't let me down.
216. You gotta give me a sign.
217. Will you be ready when I call?
218. Don't look behind you.
219. I see a great tragedy in your future.
220. Yes, I've been crying.
221. I can't deny how I feel about you.
222. I created you!
223. Do you know the way home?
224. I've thrown it all away.
225. I didn't mean to make you cry.
226. Nothing really matters anyway.
227. I've got to face the truth.
228. She sends shivers down my spine.
229. I'm going straight to hell.
230. Suck the poison out!
231. So you think you can just love me and leave me?
232. The cops are going to be here in a few minutes.
233. Anytime you need me, just call.
234. Explain to me why I dream of you every night.
235. I want you to kill her.
236. I need to ask you an important question.

237. What's ya gonna do once the walls start crumbling in?
238. Thanks for listening.
239. Please tell me that you're not wearing that.
240. Dude, that's not funny.
241. We're gonna have to find a place to hide the body.
242. Please don't kill me.
243. Come on, baby, it's my birthday.
244. I poisoned your drink.
245. Problems sleeping?
246. I've been a very bad girl.
247. I'm going to go blow my brains out.
248. They're going to arrest me for sending you that picture.
249. We're not going to make it out alive.
250. I've always loved you.
251. People are counting on you to save them.
252. Why won't you marry me?
253. Why won't you kiss me?
254. We have to end this affair immediately.
255. I wish I had your body.
256. You've changed.
257. The aliens killed her.
258. Why did I think you ever deserved me?
259. I'm going to go fight in the war.
260. It'd be nice if you could show a little kindness from time to time.
261. Get on your knees punk!
262. Get your act together.
263. Come on, take a drink.
264. I didn't mean to turn you on.
265. Let's run away and be together forever.
266. We're not going to make it out alive.
267. Is this our claim to fame?
268. What did you do to your hair?
269. They're playing our song.
270. Let's sit down and be serious for a moment.

Scene Starters

Here both parties on stage will know the scene, but no dialogue is specifically stated. The scene should not start until both parties are prepared to begin the scene.

1. This is a couple at the end of a first date.
2. Newlywed couple watching the snow fall on Christmas.
3. A pirate capturing a young wench.
4. A prince and princess sharing a ballroom dance.
5. A drunk chick hitting on an old guy in a bar.
6. A man's daughter telling him that she's marrying a man she just met.
7. A man finds his daughter packing her bags because she's dropping out of college to join the Peace Corps in Africa.
8. An old man begging for food outside a coffee shop.
9. A woman goes into labor and the cabbie has to deliver the baby.
10. A father physically abusing his daughter.
11. A woman breaking up with her boyfriend.
12. The actor and actress have been fighting before their big, romantic scene.
13. The man is secretly in love with the woman.
14. The man and woman are trapped in a cave during a storm.
15. A daughter is giving a kidney to her estranged father.
16. Daughter is trying to help her dad through a bout of depression.
17. A man breaks into a convenience store to rob the woman behind the counter.
18. Father trying to comfort his newly paralyzed daughter.
19. The daughter found her father cheating on her mother.
20. Father and grown daughter meeting for the first time.
21. The man is a vampire about to taste the blood of another victim.
22. The woman has made a special meal for her man in hopes of winning him back.

Beginning Scenes

These scenes are used to help provide initial guidance and motivation for beginning and intermediate actors and actresses. These scenes vary and are for 1-4 people. (*You are permitted to copy the Beginning Scenes and Long Scenes pages from this book, but for rehearsal use only. They may not be used for any performances, whether you charge admission or not. The photocopies are to be destroyed after you have completed using them.* Tip… Cut out each character from the photocopy and give it to each actor.) Do not announce what each character has on their sheet. Give each actor their own sheet so they will not know the motivation or actions of their scene partner. The key to this exercise is to go with your own actions, but react and adapt to the scene as it progresses. There is no set ending to these scenes. Let them progress as any real situation would.

Scene 1

MAN - Enough is enough. She keeps putting you off. You've been nice and considerate and everything she's asked for. You've even let her date other guys to "make sure you're the one". But now it's time for her to commit to this relationship or you're walking.

FEMALE - You two have been dating (sort of, according to him) for a few months. He has been asking for you to commit to an exclusive relationship. But why do that? You've got guys out there who you haven't dated yet. But you might risk losing him and why would you want to do that? He's always there for you when you're lonely or bored. Just one question: "Why can't he better looking?"

Scene 2

MAN 1– You caught your girlfriend, FEMALE at the movie theater with MAN 2. She had told you she was going to hang out at the mall with FEMALE.

FEMALE – You went behind your boyfriend, MAN 1's back and went on a date at the movies with MAN 2. It was an especially wonderful day with a very special guy.

MAN 2– You just spent a Saturday afternoon at the movies with FEMALE. It was an especially wonderful day with a very special young lady.

Scene 3

MAN – You can't take it anymore. FEMALE is driving you crazy. Crazy in love, that is. It's time to ask her out on a date.

FEMALE – You have been flirting with MAN for a long time trying to get his attention. It finally seems like it's working. But the director of the theater doesn't allow dating between students. But he is so funny and cute and you really want to date him. At least once. But if the director finds out, you'll both be out of drama!

Scene 4

MAN – You are homeless. But you're not a bad person. A string of bad luck has landed you in this situation. You're cold, hungry, and all hope seems lost. And you're desperate enough to break into a house with this gun.

FEMALE – It's a nice quiet evening. Very relaxing. You're hungry so you head into the kitchen to make a sandwich.

Scene 5

FEMALE - You're trapped inside a cave. It's dark and storming outside. You are deathly afraid of storms. The guy next to you used to be your boyfriend, but he couldn't show any emotion.

MAN - You're trapped inside a cave. It's dark and storming outside. The girl next to you used to be your girlfriend. But she dumped you because you couldn't show any cmotion.

Scene 6

FEMALE 1- You are in your bedroom packing. It's a small suitcase, so deciding what to take is difficult. Leaving home always is. Your parents are unbearable. Aren't you old enough to make your own decisions? Like who you will or won't date. You are in love with a young man. You're going to go be with him forever.

FEMALE 2- You hear a commotion in your sister's room. She was upset earlier, so go check on her and find out why.

Scene 7

FEMALE 1 - You kneel beside some young thug. A gun is pointed at your head. You stole something from them and they want it back. But they don't know that you definitely took it.

FEMALE 2 - You hold a gun a gun to the person kneeling beside you. You suspect they stole something from you. And if they don't return it, you're going to kill them.

Scene 8

MAN 1 – You are watching a very romantic movie with the girl (FEMALE 1) next to you. She's pretty and it took a lot of courage to ask her out. You don't know if she really likes you or just went out with you to see the movie. You'd like to hold her hand, but then she might think you're creepy.

FEMALE 2 – You are watching a very romantic movie with MAN 1. You don't really care for him that much. You were bored and wanted to go to the movies. Plus he paid. That's good.

MAN 2– You are watching a very romantic movie with the girl (FEMALE 2) next to you. She's pretty and it took a lot of courage to ask her out. But you really like the other girl (FEMALE 1) next to you. You went on this double date just to be close to her. You'd like to hold her hand, but it's too risky. Maybe you could sneak a little contact in when no one's looking.

FEMALE 2 – You are watching a very romantic movie with the guy (MAN 2) next to you. You've had a crush on him for a long time. You would really love him to hold your hand.

Scene 9 (Solo scene)

FEMALE – You're hungry. You look in the refrigerator, but all that's in there is beer and moldy cheese. Your dad promised he'd bring some food home, but he's late. He's always late. And it's been this way for weeks. He rarely works and when he does, he spends all the money on beer and cigarettes.

Scene 10

FEMALE – You are at the steps to your house. It's the end of a wonderful date with MAN. He was a perfect gentleman. You went out for dinner and a movie. One that you picked out. He didn't try to hold your hand. He didn't even try to get too close to you. In fact he was so nice and perfect that you're actually thinking of giving him a goodnight kiss.

MAN – You are at the steps of FEMALE's house. It's the end of a wonderful date with her. You were a perfect gentleman. You went out for dinner and a movie. One that she picked out. You didn't try to hold her hand. You didn't even try to get too close to her. You would like a goodnight kiss, but you aren't going to ask for one.

Scene 11

FEMALE 1- You are in a hospital bed. In a few minutes, the nurses will come and take you back for your operation. You're having a kidney transplant. If it's successful, it'll save your life. Right next to you is one of your closest friends. They're giving their kidney to you. This operation is a risk for them too. If something goes wrong, they could die.

FEMALE 2 - You are in a hospital bed. In a few minutes, the nurses will come and take you back for an operation. You're giving one of your kidney's to one of your closest friends. If it's successful, it'll save their life. But if something goes wrong, you could die.

Scene 12

FEMALE 1 – You're walking through the woods. It started out nice, but the sun is beginning to set. You and your friends haven't been able to find the rest of your camping party and FEMALE 3 is getting on your nerves.

FEMALE 2 - You're walking through the woods. It started out nice, but the sun is beginning to set. You and your friends haven't been able to find the rest of your camping party and you're afraid you won't find them. You haven't eaten in hours. You're thirsty and you're feet are really aching.

FEMALE 3 - You're walking through the woods. It started out nice, but the sun is beginning to set. You and your friends haven't been able to find the rest of your camping party. You love the adventure. Maybe you'll have to look all night. No problem. You'll have some good stories to tell. FEMALE 2 is freaking out a bit and you feel like pushing her buttons even more.

Scene 13

MAN – There is a girl in class that you have your heart set on. She's been nothing but a perfect lady to you. Always a friend. Always encouraging you. She has no idea you feel this way about her. But you know you have to tell her. (Pick her out from the girls in class.)

Scene 14

FEMALE – There is a guy in class that you have your heart set on. He's been nothing but a perfect gentleman to you. Always a friend. Always encouraging you. He has no idea you feel this way about him. But you know you have to tell him. (Pick him out from the guys in class.)

Scene 15 (Solo scene)

MAN - You are all alone. You have been for weeks. Maybe it's been months. You don't have anyone to talk to except yourself. Food is running short. There seems to be no escape from this island. Unless death counts.

Scene 16

FEMALE - As you sit in your wheelchair and come to the realization that you'll never walk again, the dances you'll never dance with your boyfriend (MAN), the walks on the beach with your newlywed husband that will never happen, and the bike rides with your children that will never be, come flooding in. All this because you refused to wear a seat belt while riding in the car and when the accident happened, you were thrown from the car.

MAN – FEMALE, your girlfriend of the past year was in a horrible car accident. She survived, but will never walk again. If you two are going to have a continuing relationship, you're going to have to decide if you are willing to help take care of her. She'll never dance and you love to dance. She'll never be able to go for walks or bike rides like you two used to do all the time. You have to ask yourself if it's worth it. Or is time to break it off and move on.

Scene 17

MAN - All you want is a kiss. Sure you walk with a limp and stutter when you talk, but you would like to know what it's like to kiss a girl before you die. And you have just one night left before you die. No one knows and you won't tell them. You don't want anyone to have sympathy for you. But if you can get the girl to kiss you, you'll die happy.

Scene 18

MAN – You and FEMALE have been dating for months. You are deeply in love with her. You want to hold her hand, put your arm around her, and kiss her. You want to show your woman off to the world. You are so proud to have her as your girlfriend. All you seem to be able to talk about is the day you two will be married.

FEMALE – You and MAN have been dating for a long time. You love him, but the passion is gone. He's your friend and boyfriend, but the desire to hold his hand or kiss him has long faded. So much so, that you think it's time to move on.

Scene 19

FEMALE – You found a bottle on the floor. Rub it. Who knows what might happen.

MALE – You are the genie from the bottle. Give the FEMALE three wishes. But they can only happen within the drama room and only you can make them happen. With the help of the great and powerful genie. (your director)

Scene 20

MAN – You are in love. Not just in love, but madly, passionately, illogically, miserably, all-consumingly in love, with a young woman (FEMALE).

FEMALE - You've seen this person before, and have a vague recollection of his face. But you have less than a passing interest in them.

Scene 21

FEMALE – You are going to be handed a poem by FEMALE 2. She didn't write it. She knows who did, but is sworn to secrecy. You need to know. You must know. Beat it out of her if you have to.

FEMALE – You were given this poem by a MAN (A guy from class). He asked you to give it to FEMALE 1. You sneaked a peak at it. It's beautiful. He swore you to secrecy so you can't tell her it's from him. He will beat you to a pulp if you tell her.

POEM
Within the eyes and tussled hair
Lie beauty unknown to men of past
Shall only God know what will come
For those who wait and those who last

We live and breathe to hope and dream
Within this life our true one will see
What love can bring when faith abounds
Surely as the souls in heaven be

I ask you now before I fall
As friends and tortured souls often will
Love, hold me, and live forever
In the arms of angels wings so still

Scene 22 (Solo scene)

MALE or FEMALE – Crap! You were supposed to be taking care of your friend's dog this week. But you forgot. Get over there quick. Though it's likely too late. The dog is probably already rotting in the sun. How are you going to explain this?

Scene 23

FEMALE 1 - The music has just started. You love this song. It's so romantic. Now is your time to grab that guy you've been wanting to dance with, but he's been too shy to ask you. So take charge and pull him out there for this dance. Before it's too late.

FEMALE 2 - The music has just started. You love this song. It's so romantic. Now is your time to grab that guy you've been wanting to dance with, but he's been too shy to ask you. So take charge and pull him out there for this dance. Before it's too late.

MAN - The music has just started. You love this song. It's so romantic. Now is your time to grab that girl you've been wanting to dance with, but you've been too shy to ask her. So take charge and pull her out there for this dance. Before it's too late.

Scene 24

MALE – Now is your time to let her know how you feel. It's time to lay it all out on the table and tell FEMALE how you feel about her. How you lie awake at night and when you do sleep, you dream of her. The feelings are eating you up inside and you need to know if there is any chance she might feel the same about you.

FEMALE - Now is your time to let him know how you feel. It's time to lay it all out on the table and tell MALE how you feel about him. How you lie awake at night and when you do sleep, you dream of him. The feelings are eating you up inside and you need to know if there is any chance he might feel the same about you.

Scene 25

FEMALE – You're pregnant. And if that wasn't bad enough, you don't know who the father is. Maybe it's MAN 1. Maybe it's MAN 2. Or it might be MAN 3. You should probably get them all together and break the news to them. (Pick 3 guys from class.)

Scene 26

MAN 1 - You have no idea who you are or how you got where you are. No one else looks familiar to you. You want to escape but there appears to be no way out except for the door, and it's locked.

FEMALE 1 - You have no idea who you are or how you got where you are. This guy doesn't look familiar to you. You like it here. You have been here for days and somehow have never been hungry or thirsty.

FEMALE 2 - You have no idea who you are or how you got where you are. This MAN doesn't look familiar to you. He must have appeared while you were sleeping. You want to escape but there appears to be no way out except for the door, and it's locked. You have been here for days and somehow have never been hungry or thirsty.

FEMALE 3 - You have no idea who you are or how you got where you are. No one else looks familiar to you. You want to escape but there appears to be no way out except for the door, and it's locked. You have been here for days and somehow have never been hungry or thirsty. You were the first one in this room. The others have magically appeared one at a time over the past several days whenever you wake from your sleeping.

Scene 27

FEMALE – You're sick of all the crap going on. You're sick of that loser MAN cheating on you again. You hate FEMALE for stealing him. You're sick of the girls making fun of you. You're sick of life. So now it's time to end a few. Take this gun and make MAN and FEMALE know how you feel. Then kill them. And then kill yourself. Let everyone see what they did to you. (Pick a guy and girl from class.)

Scene 28

FEMALE - Two weeks ago, you and MAN made a big decision. A huge decision. And now you are about to pay the consequences of your actions. You just found out that you are pregnant. You are going to keep the baby. Is MAN going stand up and be the father he should be?

MAN - FEMALE has called you over to talk about something.

Scene 29

MAN 1 – You're drunk. Again! It's fun. You got your connections. You have the money. Getting beer is easier than you thought. And it takes the pain away. The pain that FEMALE caused when she dumped you. The only bad side effect is that you keep hearing MAN 2's voice ringing through your brain.

MAN 2 – You are voice in the head of MAN 1. Every so often make random statements directed at him. And throw in some rude ones.

Scene 30

FEMALE 1 – You are the star! The star of your own television program. You can't go anywhere without people recognizing you. Everyone wants your autograph. Problem is that you don't like people. They're stupid and annoy you. Why don't they just leave you alone?

FEMALE 2 – OMG, it's FEMALE 1! Your favorite actress in the whole world. You never miss her show. You know everything about it. You can't believe she's right there in front of you. So don't be shy. This opportunity may never happen again.

Scene 31

FEMALE 1– You are about to be executed for crimes against humanity. You questioned the leader (FEMALE 2) of this desolate world. A world run only by teenagers since all the adults died. You have only minutes until your life will end.

FEMALE 2 – You are the leader of a desolate world run by teenagers. All the adults died a mysterious death. You rule with an iron fist. All must obey you. And if anyone questions you, they must pay with their life. Like FEMALE 1, who questioned your authority.

FEMALE - You live in a desolate world run by teenagers. All the adults died a mysterious death. You obey your leader FEMALE 2 at all costs. You do as she says without question. She has appointed you executioner and your first execution is to be FEMALE 1 who questioned FEMALE 2's authority. Remove her from her cell and bring justice to this world.

Scene 32

FEMALE 1 – You are a nerd. A major nerd. You're quiet and reserved. It's because you hide a secret. You have a temper and can blow up at people if you don't control it.

FEMALE 2 - You are the class bully. You love to make yourself feel better by picking on the weak and scared. The more scared they get, the harder you get on them. Take no prisoners. Beat their spirits into the ground. Rule the world. It's yours take it.

Scene 33

FEMALE 1 – You're stranded in a lifeboat somewhere out on the ocean. No sign of land anywhere. You're tired, thirsty, and very hungry. You and your two fellow survivors haven't eaten in nearly two weeks. If you don't eat soon you will all die. Someone is going to have to make the ultimate sacrifice so that two can have a chance to eat their flesh and survive.

FEMALE 2 – You're stranded in a lifeboat somewhere out on the ocean. No sign of land anywhere. You're tired, thirsty, and very hungry. You and your two fellow survivors haven't eaten in nearly two weeks. If you don't eat soon you will all die. Someone is going to have to make the ultimate sacrifice so that two can have a chance to eat their flesh and survive.

FEMALE – You're stranded in a lifeboat somewhere out on the ocean. No sign of land anywhere. You're tired, thirsty, and very hungry. You and your two fellow survivors haven't eaten in nearly two weeks. If you don't eat soon you will all die. Someone is going to have to make the ultimate sacrifice so that two can have a chance to eat their flesh and survive.

Scene 34

MAN 1 – It's a normal day for you. Just you and MAN 2 hanging out talking about guy stuff. Until any girl gets close to you. Then you get nervous. Your ability to speak clear and understandable sentences suddenly goes away. You are afraid they'll think you're a loser and an idiot.

MAN 2 - It's a normal day for you. Just you and MAN 1 hanging out talking about guy stuff. You know he isn't comfortable around girls, so you want to help him find a nice girl to date. There are several to choose from in drama, but FEMALE 1 has the highest chance of actually of actually going out with him.

FEMALE – You don't know what it is, but MAN 1 attracts you. Sure he's shy, but he's kinda cute. You may have to make the first move.

Scene 35

MAN – You're at an Italian restaurant waiting for your blind date FEMALE 1 to arrive. A friend set you up with her. Supposedly she's really hot and loves funny guys. You need to impress her. Try to be funny.

FEMALE – You're going to meet your blind date at the local Italian restaurant. A friend set you up. He's supposed to be really cute. Not that it matters. You haven't had a date in over a year. So make it count. Laugh at his jokes. Don't let him get away!!!

FEMALE – You're a waitress in an Italian restaurant. It isn't busy and you see the guy (MAN) you've had a crush on sitting at one of your tables. If you play this right, maybe you'll get a lot more than a $4 tip. Wink, wink.

Scene 36

FEMALE – Why won't he leave? You can't push him out the door. He is your boyfriend after all. But you need him gone. Your secret lover is coming over soon. The thought of him makes your heart jump. You're going to attack him as soon as he walks through that door.

MAN 1 – It's been a great afternoon with your girl, FEMALE. But you've got homework to do. You should probably go. It'd be a lot more fun to study together though. Maybe you can head home, get your books, and come back.

MAN 2 – As soon as MAN 1 leaves you are in there. Don't let him see you though. This is a secret meeting. There won't be much talking though. Just action. Go get her tiger!!!

Scene 37

MAN - You live in a destroyed world where only one other person exists. That person is across the room from you. But that person is also your sworn enemy. You will survive at all costs.

FEMALE - You live in a destroyed world where only one other person exists. That person is across the room from you. But that person is also your sworn enemy. You will survive at all costs.

Long Scenes for the Whole Class

After spending time working on your "yes, anding…" and doing several weeks of the short scenes it's time to try your hand at the long scenes. But before we go there, we're going to play a little game we call "Society". Before you start, you'll need a deck of playing cards. Use enough cards from the deck so that there are a few more cards than performers. Each class member is going to draw a card from your stack. They should not show it to anyone!!! The rank of the card signifies their status in Society. For our purposes, we use a medieval society, but any genre of time can work. Here is an example of how ranking of the cards relates to the ranking in society:

King – The King obviously
Queen - The Queen obviously
Jack – The son (or daughter) of the King and Queen or someone of nobility
10 – Priest, or lesser nobility
9 – Perhaps the town sheriff or someone of importance.
8 – A more wealthy shopkeeper. Probably owns some land.
7 - A shopkeeper
6 – A shopkeeper
5 – Perhaps a farmer or poor merchant
4 – A lowly commoner or perhaps the town crier.
3 – Perhaps a thief
2 – A homeless person who sleeps under a bridge
Ace – A homeless person without a bridge to sleep under

By no means does this mean that you must portray the characters as I've listed them here. This is simply the way we've done it. Adjust it to meet the needs of your theater group. Understand that there will be times when a guy may draw the Queen and/or a young lady may draw the King. That's fine. They play the character they draw, regardless of gender.

Scenes of this nature can run from 30-60 or more minutes depending on the complexity of the scene and the ability of the players. You can choose to employ props and set pieces if you want. We have done it with and without and both work equally well. We have also done this scene as caveman, the Roman Empire, an Old West town, and a futuristic society. I'm sure with some thought, you can come up with many more societies of your own. Leave me some feedback. We'd love to give them a try.

After you've played Society a few times, it's time to move onto more directed scenes. In all of these scenes, props ARE encouraged. Items may need to be scavenged. Sets built in advance or during the scene. Only imagination and money will limit your abilities. You can add or subtract characters as needed for each scene. These are simply starting points for you.

Long Scene 1- The Rocket Ship

Has it been 9 months already? This is what happens when you're scrambling to save a few human beings. Only 3 months ago, a small band of scientists discovered a large astcroid hurtling toward earth. Our earth is about to be destroyed. So, you've worked day and night building a spaceship that will take a handful of people from earth. For your efforts, you have a 50-50 chance of being one of those who will get to fly on that spaceship. Tonight you will draw lots to see who will win the right to live. Or at least have a chance to live. Unfortunately, death awaits the unlucky ones once the asteroid hits the earth and destroys it. But that is still three days away and for now there is still work to be done. The ship isn't quite finished. And the last of the supplies need to be loaded onboard for tomorrow's journey.

Lead scientist – You discovered the asteroid and made the arrangements for the ship to be built. For that, you have a guaranteed spot on the spaceship.

Billionaire – You're old. Very old. And very wealthy. It was your money that bought all the supplies and materials for this spaceship. Your money has bought you a spot on the spaceship and thus saved your life.

Commander – Your flying expertise is second to none. Because of that, you have a guaranteed spot on the spaceship. Your fiancé however, doesn't have a guaranteed spot.

Doctor – You must perform checks on everyone to ensure that they can survive the spaceflight. And a doctor will be needed once they land on their new planet. For that, you have a guaranteed spot on the spaceship.

Lead Foreman – It's your job to make sure the spaceship is finished. Lead your team and hurry. For your efforts, you will be allowed to draw two lots from the hat. This should increase your chances of being selected for the flight.

Supply Manager – Make sure all supplies are placed onboard. Check your lists. Nothing can be forgotten. Lead your team and hurry. For your efforts, you will be allowed to draw two lots from the hat. This should increase your chances of being selected for the flight.

Boyfriend – No matter what happens tonight when the lots are drawn, you aren't going if your girlfriend isn't going. You will live together or die together.

Girlfriend – No matter what happens tonight when the lots are drawn, you aren't going if your boyfriend isn't going. You will live together or die together.

Fiancé - You are the Commander's future wife. He is going to fly the spaceship. You have been working hard yourself on this spaceship, but your spot is not guaranteed like his is.

Long Scene 2 - Old Town

The year is 1859. Times they are a changin'. People are talking about a war coming between the Yankees and the good people of the south. The railroad recently started making stops in your town and that has made the city grow. Of course, you still know everybody. It isn't that big of a town. Except for the occasional stranger who wanders into town. And that's the one you gotta watch out for. You gotta find out if he's one of those Yankees.

Mayor – You're well liked. And those that don't like you are "encouraged" to move. Always a smile on your face and a hand in someone else's business. Especially the ones that will get you bribe or two. Now how are you going to get the tax collector to pay you?!

Sheriff – You are the law! This is your town and it's going to stay free of the scum. You welcome strangers as long as they obey the laws and you've got a soft spot for people down on their luck.

Drunk – 'Nuff said. You also love to gamble. Maybe you can find a game somewhere.

Thief – You and the sheriff are good buddies. You became good friends because of all the times you've been caught stealing from the shops in town.

Deputy – Dumb as they come and you do whatever the Sheriff says. Unless you get near your heartthrob, the clothes maker. You're ability to think and speak clearly goes right out the window.

Baker – Everyone sees you for fresh bread. You are loved by all. Except the sheriff.

Tax Collector – It's tax time and everyone has to pay their fair share. You skim a little off the top to pay for your gambling addiction.

Stranger – You appear normal. Friendly. Smiling. But you have a secret. You're a Yankee. If they find out they'll drive you out of town. But you have something better for them. A chance to turn the clock ahead.

Blacksmith – You are possibly the busiest person in town. Always taking care of the horses. There is never a day of rest. But times may get rough if the scientist latest invention actually works.

Farmer – You need your horse's shoes fixed and you need some supplies, but money is tight right now. The kids are hungry. Maybe the shopkeepers will let you slide on paying them until the harvest.

Banker – You're wealthy and always willing to lend money. But you ain't giving it away. They need collateral and you got to charge interest.

Laborer – You got no skills that you're great at, but you can do ok at some jobs. You haven't eaten in a couple days. You've got to find some work today.

Doctor – You're old and have been the doctor in this town for nearly 40 years. You've seen every one of the townspeople naked at one time or another. You've delivered all their children. You know every ailment of every person. And you ain't afraid to tell people.

Shopkeeper – You make clothes. Work clothes, dresses, boots. Watch the deputy real close. He's trying to bust your gambling operation you run from the back of the shop.

Long Scene 3 - Old Town (Part 2)

The year is 1880. The Civil War is a distant past, though many in the south think they'll rise again. Even now, the rednecks are starting to be born. Times they are a changin' though. The railroad recently started making stops in your town and that has made the city grow. Of course, you still know everybody. It isn't that big of a town. Except for the occasional stranger who wanders into town. And that's the onc you gotta watch out for.

Mayor – You're well liked. And those that don't like you are "encouraged" to move. Always a smile on your face and a hand in someone else's business. Especially the ones that will get you bribe or two. Now how are you going to get the tax collector to pay you?!

Sheriff – You are the law! This is your town and it's going to stay free of the scum. You welcome strangers as long as they obey the laws and you've got a soft spot for people down on their luck except the banker. NO good conniving...

Drunk – 'Nuff said. You also love to gamble. Maybe you can find a game somewhere.

Thief – You and the sheriff are good buddies. You became good friends because of all the times you've been caught stealing from the shops in town.

Deputy – Dumb as they come and you do whatever the Sheriff says. Unless you get near your heartthrob, the clothes maker. You're ability to think and speak clearly goes right out the window.

Baker – Everyone sees you for fresh bread. You are loved by all. Except the sheriff.

Stranger – You appear normal. Friendly. Smiling. But you have a secret. A secret that will change these people's lives.

Scientist – You're always working on inventions. Most are junk, but if this new one works out, horses will be obsolete. You call it the automobile.

Blacksmith – You are possibly the busiest person in town. Always taking care of the horses. There is never a day of rest. But times may get rough if the scientist latest invention actually works.

Tax Collector – It's tax time and everyone has to pay their fair share. You skim a little off the top to pay for your gambling addiction.

Farmer – You need your horse's shoes fixed and you need some supplies, but money is tight right now. The kids are hungry. Maybe the shopkeepers will let you slide on paying them until the harvest.

Banker – You're wealthy and always willing to lend money. But you ain't giving it away. They need collateral and you got to charge interest.

Doctor – You're old and have been the doctor in this town for nearly 40 years. You've seen every one of the townspeople naked at one time or another. You've delivered all their children. You know every ailment of every person. And you ain't afraid to tell people.

Shopkeeper – You make clothes. Work clothes, dresses, boots. Watch the deputy real close. He's trying to bust your gambling operation you run from the back of the shop.

Long Scene 4 - Post Nuclear War Survival

The year is 2040. It's been 15 years since World War 3 ended. More than 500 million people died in the war. More than a billion have died since the nuclear winter set in following the war. Famine has forced people to beg, borrow, or steal whatever is necessary to survive. Everyone longs for the good days. But there is little hope. People simply exist. There is no joy anymore. Your leader, General Marshall, has promised a better future. He has promised that all would have food and clean water on every table. You've heard this from others before, but they couldn't deliver. General Marshall has. But in turn, proper behavior is mandatory. Laws must be obeyed no matter how trivial they are. Sheriff Sammons and Judge Adams will preside over the laws of the land. Or be prepared to face the executioner.

Dictator (General Marshall) – Most people believe your words that great things are coming. Sure food gets delivered from time to time. (There's plenty stored in a secret hiding place.) And the water is slightly better than it used to be. (Yet, you drink bottled water, since you have all that's left over from the war.) Little do they know that you are willing to sacrifice your people for your own gains. You will sell them to the highest bidder. All so that you can maintain control. You must rule this land. It is your destiny!!! You have heard rumors that a rebel leader is trying to undermine your authority. Find this person and have them put to death before you lose your power. Remember that only Judge Adams can sentence someone to death. But since the Judge wants to stay in a position of power, you're sure they'll do as you ask. Use the Town Crier to make all announcements. It is illegal for your government workers to give their extra food to the common townspeople.

Sheriff Sammons – You are the law! You enforce every law that General Marshall lays down. No matter what it is. Any who disobey are either thrown in prison or taking to the judge for sentencing. Use the Town Crier to make all announcements.

Judge Adams – It is your job to pass either guilt or innocence on the people of the land. And if you want to keep your job, you'll do just as Sheriff Sammons says. Or else they may pass it on to General Marshall that you've gone soft. You don't want to be starving again. Use the Town Crier to make all announcements. It is illegal for government workers to give their extra food to the common townspeople.

Executioner – You know all the people of this town. They are your friends. Your children go to school with their children. But the law is the law and if you want to have a job and provide food for your family, then you're going to have to be willing to do your job. Even if it means bringing the axe down on your friends necks. It is illegal for government workers to give their extra food to the common townspeople.

Town Crier – You make all announcements for the General, Sheriff, and Judge. The more you do for them, the more they will reward you. You are fortunate that they picked you from the common town people. It is illegal to give your extra food to your friends, but you sure do want to help them.

Farmer – You are able to raise a few vegetables on what little land you farm. You can choose to keep it for you and your family or share it with 2 friends. But only 2.

Fisherman – You were able to catch a 2 small fish today. This is big news for all the starving people.

Rebel leader – You know General Marshall is ruthless and bad. You must find a way to convince the others and remove the General, Sheriff, and Judge from their positions. But this may cost you, your family, and friends their lives. Plan carefully. If word gets out, you'll surely lose your head. You need to recruit spies to find out where General Marshall is hiding the supplies.

Baker – You are one of the lucky ones. General Marshall provides you with enough material to feed 4 customers each day. You need to find someone to try and get more wheat from the grain bin so that you can make more bread. But if anyone gets caught... well you know the consequences.

Townsperson – Your best friend is dying. They are coughing and have a fever. Even though you're hungry and thirsty, you must find a doctor or your friend will die.

Townsperson – You are starving. Maybe there will be food today.

Townsperson – You are starving. Maybe there will be food today. If not, you're going to steal some. Provided you have the energy.

Townsperson – It's your job to build a fire. Maybe there will be bread or a little meat to eat today.

Townsperson – You believe that better days are coming. You had a vision that someone would come and deliver you and your friends from this horrible famine and despair. Or maybe it was another delusion from the heat and lack of water.

Doctor – Your supplies are limited. There isn't much you can do for people other than ease their suffering before death takes them.

Stranger – You have come from a land far away. A land where there is food and water and people can lead normal lives. A place where people live in houses and have their freedom.

Tribe leader – You control a group of people that live across the mountains. The women in your group have been dying off and you need to bring some others back with you. Perhaps you can work out a deal with General Marshall.

Long Scene 5 - Fire and Ice

No one remembers when it happened. Maybe it was five hundred years ago. Maybe it was two thousand years. Who knows? But everyone knows that a day used to be 24 hours long. And then the Earth was hit by an asteroid and its orbit changed. Now the Earth is like the moon used to be. There is only day or night. One side always faces the sun and one side is always facing away. The side facing the sun is so hot that no food can grow. The people living there, in the area known as the Barren land, can only venture out when the clouds cover the sun because there is no night. Rain rarely ever falls and when it does, the people rejoice. The people living on the dark side, known as the Frozen land, never see daylight. Their land is covered in ice and snow. Warmth is something that they have never known. But between these lands of contrast and their struggles to survive is a land rich in its abundance. Only 7 miles wide, but full of green lands and beautiful springs is where the Great Ruler lives. Only the richest and most powerful people are allowed to live in the Green land under the laws of the Great Ruler. According to legend, the Green land was used to separate the Barren people from the Frozen people for the years had greatly changed each one. They no longer spoke the same language. It was feared that should the two ever meet, then their diseases might kill all of them and perhaps even those living in the Green land. And so it has been for many years that for as long as anyone can remember, it has been forbidden for the Barren people and the Frozen people to enter the Green land. As long as that is obeyed, then the Great Ruler will supply each land with enough supplies to survive.

Great Ruler – You know the truth. Your land is only 7 miles wide. There is not enough room for all the Barren people and Frozen people to live in your small land. So you must make them fear each other. You do supply them with meager rations that allow them to survive, but that's it. Too much and they might have the strength to take over your land. It is nearly time to call for each tribe to send their respective sacrifice to you. (They think they're being sacrificed. Actually you use them as slaves. Offer them servitude in place of death.)

Barren people – You wear few clothes because of the heat. Your skin is dark. Your eyes are small to help block the sun's light. You live in caves. You must rely on the Great Ruler to supply all your needs. You can grow no food. Water is only turned on for one hour a day. You must use it quickly before it evaporates in the heat. Your language is done almost as if you're singing. The sound of each word rises and falls like a rollercoaster. Choose who will be your ancestral leader. They should be not only wise. Today you will learn five new words of your ancestral language.

Frozen people – Your land is always dark and cold. You must be bundled up constantly, except when in your small one room houses. Wood is scarce and must be used for fires, so houses are small. Near the Green land is a small area where fish can be caught. All other supplies are given to you by the Great Ruler. The cold are has damaged your vocal cords. Your sounds of your voices are lower and you speak slowly. Choose who will be your ancestral leader. They must be wise, but also a female. Today you will learn five new words of your ancestral language.

Barren leader – You are the old wise one. It is your job to assign tasks. Remind your tribe that there is great danger near the Green land. Rumors are spreading that the barbarians from the Frozen land have been venturing into the Green land. Supposedly, the Frozen people have a great hatred of the Barren people. Legend says that Frozen people kill Barren people and eat them if they get the chance and use their skins as blankets. And you must teach the language of your ancestors. Everyone must memorize every word. It is the way of your people. Today's lesson includes the following words:

hand – pyka va	girl – villa sor
finger(s)– nan ba(n)	head – la man wa
touch – kelli mor	see – char di
love – sentu	go – dee tu
kiss – noen so	kill – gini ta

The Great Ruler has ordered you to send one female into the Green land. She is to be sacrificed. This is the tradition of this land. It is preferred that a female volunteer for this sacrifice. If no one is willing to go, The Great Ruler will cut off all necessary supplies. The tribe would not survive. So you must send one, even by force, if necessary.

Frozen leader – You are the old wise one. It is your duty to assign tasks. Rumors are spreading that the barbarians from the Barren land have been venturing into the Green land. It is known that The Barren people kill your people for no reason other than they are jealous of the fish you eat. And you must teach the language of your ancestors. Everyone must memorize every word. It is the way of your people. Today's lesson includes the following words:

hand – manu	boy – punka
fingers – vintus	face – tumba
touch – runkas	eyes – buntos
love – lufdum	escape – rugutum
kiss – kusp	die - hurman

The Great Ruler has ordered you to send one male into the Green land. He is to be sacrificed. It is the tradition of this land and the male you choose must go freely. If no one is willing to go, The Great Ruler will cut off all necessary supplies. The tribe would not survive. So you must send one, even by force, if necessary.

Chosen Female – Your sacrifice will ensure the continued survival of your tribe. You will be remembered in song and stories for many years to come. Go to your death with your head held high.

Chosen Male - Your sacrifice will ensure the continued survival of your tribe. You will be remembered in song and stories for many years to come. You are not afraid of death, but do not believe that the Great Ruler is any better than you. Human life is too important to just throw away. Use your intelligence and wit to save yourself. You can't do this alone. You will need to find someone to assist you.

Long Scene 6 - Slave Ship

The year is 1791. The United States is growing after winning its freedom from England. But labor is needed. In particular, cheap labor is wanted. And this has led to a booming slave trade. Demand is high and so are the prices. The slave ship, Mary Elizabeth, has just arrived on the west coast of Africa. The crew's job is to capture as many Negroes as possible and take them back to America.

Captain – You get paid well to transport slaves though you are personally against slavery.

First mate – You love your job. You don't think there's anything wrong with slavery. Blacks are inferior to whites anyway. But you don't like seeing blacks mistreated. You need them all alive so that you can make more money once you return to America.

Deckhand – You help capture the slaves in Africa and you work on the ship. You enjoy tormenting the captured slaves.

Deckhand – Slavery is wrong. It goes against the laws of God. But this is your job and you will do it.

Deckhand – You've never seen a black person before. They're strange. You're curious to catch one and check them out.

Slave trader – You take the slaves from the ships and sell them to the highest bidder. Use whatever means necessary to sell each slave for the highest price you can get. You have a special "Slave buyer" that will try and build the price up. Work with them before the auction starts.

Slave capturer –Your role aboard the ship is to lead the capture of the Africans. You are ruthless. Nothing will stand in your way of taking a full ship back with you.

Plantation Owner – Your plantation needs workers. Buy as many as you can afford. Slaves are the only way to stay profitable. You are a Christian and not prone to mistreating slaves. But those who get out of line must be punished.

Slave Buyer (price driver) – Your job is to drive the price up but not so much that you win the auction. You are a tool of the Slave Trader. Make sure you work together on this.

Wife – You enjoy having the slaves to do the work of the house. Your Christian duty is to convert the slaves to Christ.

Child – You hope your dad buys you a slave child to play with.

House slave – You have been the property of the Master and Mistress of the house your entire life. They treat you well. But you're still a slave. You have long lost hope of ever being free.

Slave Master – You keep the slaves on the plantation in order. You give them their chores and you dish out punishment to those who misbehave.

Slave

Slave child

Long Scene 7 - 8 Days
(Inspired by the Ray Bradbury short story
"Fire and Frost")

Mocs - Your heart beats at more than 400 beats per minute. It's normal. It didn't used to be. It used to beat at 70 beats a minute. The solar radiation has increased everyone's heartbeat. And it's shortened everyone's life span. Your people used to live for 70, 80, 90 years. Now you are lucky to live a mere eight days. You are born, grow up, marry, have children, grow old and die all in such a short time. It doesn't seem fair. But that is fate you have been dealt. The solar radiation also makes survival outside the caves extremely difficult. The days are filled with 180 degree days. The nights filled with sub zero temperatures. Each morning you have only one hour to gather the melting frost and any plants you can. You also have one hour each evening as the sun sets to "enjoy" the world. Water and food are limited and you must share it with Walways who live high on the cliffs. Though they suffer in a world like yours, they are given a full 10 days of life because the cliffs help shield the radiation. It gives them a full two more days than you. If you can kill one and eat their heart, legend says you will live an extra day. But killing them is hard. You may die trying. Is it worth it? Before life became so short, scientists roamed the planet. There is a spaceship somewhere that can take two people to a planet where people live normal, long lives. You might even bring back a rescue party and save everyone. If you look to the east, you might see the sun glint off the metal. Many have tried to reach it. None have succeeded.

Walways - Your heart beats at more than 300 beats per minute. It's normal. It didn't used to be. It used to beat at 70 beats a minute. The solar radiation has increased everyone's heartbeat. And it's shortened everyone's life

157

span. Your people used to live for 70, 80, 90 years. Now you are lucky to live a mere ten days. You are born, grow up, marry, have children, grow old and die all in such a short time. It doesn't seem fair. But that is fate you have been dealt. The solar radiation also makes survival outside the caves extremely difficult. The days are filled with 180 degree days. The nights filled with sub zero temperatures. Each morning you have only one hour to gather the melting frost and any plants you can. You also have one hour each evening as the sun sets to "enjoy" the world. Water and food are limited and you must share it with Mocs who live in the valley caves. Though they suffer in a world like yours, they are only given a mere 8 days of life. Two less than you. Legend says that if they can kill one of you, they will live an extra day. And one extra day to them is very precious. Many will die trying.

Father – Protect your children. Raise them right. You have only 4 days of life left. Pass on any wisdom you can. You should prepare the wedding of your son.

Mother - Protect your children. Raise them right. You have only 4 days of life left. Show them the love they need. You should prepare the wedding of your son.

Elder – You have one day left to live. Teach the history of your people to the young ones so that others might know what lives your people used to live. You gather them each night to tell stories.

Elder – You have two days left to live. Teach the history of your people to the young ones so that others might know what lives your people used to live. You gather them each night to tell stories.

Priest – You preside over weddings, funerals, and other spiritual needs. You have 3 days to live.

Scientist – You only have 2 days left to live. Find a way to shield your people from the radiation. They could live extra days and then maybe someone could find a way to save your people. An extra day could mean salvation.

Scientist – You have 3, maybe 4 days left to live. Teach the bright ones about the spaceship. Teach them how if they can get inside, it makes your heartbeat slow to a normal 70 beats a minute. Once inside, people are protected from the radiation. Teach them how to make it work so that they can escape and then bring back help to rescue them all.

Son – You are not content to live a mere 8 days. You will kill one of the Ilwoys and live an extra day. And you will listen to your parents and the elders and scientists. You will find a way to live. You will have a long life with the young woman you are to marry later today.

Girl – You are about to be married to a young, strong man. He dreams of reaching a spaceship. You know it's not possible, but you let him dream.

Walway leader – Do not allow the Mogs to overrun your cliff hideouts. Kill them at all costs. Use the high cliffs to your advantage.

Walway Elder – You have one day left to live. Teach the history of your people to the young ones so that others might know what lives your people used to live. You gather them each night to tell stories of the evil Mogs and greatness of the Ilwoys.

Courtship and the Cult

(This is a scene that took place over two week's time. Though this may be the strangest scene we ever worked on, it had a profound effect on all the participants. This is best accomplished by more experienced actors who know each other very well.)

Here is **Part One:**

The year is 2185. It was determined that for the betterment of society that all marriages are arranged marriages. That does not mean love is dead. In fact it is stronger than ever. Congratulations, you have reached the marrying age of 19 and are being brought here to meet your future spouse.

Gurus Tansley (MALE) and Nadia (FEMALE) are here to guide you. The rules are simple. You are to fall in love and become engaged by the end of the first session. This shouldn't be difficult. You have been groomed by society to look forward to this day. You have dreamed of the joy that comes from being shown who your spouse will be. Will it be a man or woman? The old days of the 21st century and how they labeled people for being "straight" or "gay" no longer matter now. Why did people even worry about that to begin with? What matters is that the *Committee of Peace and Love* has picked the right person for you. That's why you have spent the past two years being evaluated. You've been put through tests. You've been perfecting your marital skills in class after class. But that is now behind you. The day is nearly here and the anticipation grows. With this comes great responsibility. Divorce has not been seen for nearly 100 years. Your loyalty to your spouse and to society is of the utmost importance.

Follow their lead. They will teach you. They will guide you. Remember that true love and romance starts within one's self and radiates outward. Look into the eyes of the one chosen for you. You will see how much they love you. They want you. They have the same dreams of happiness that you do. When you meet your future spouse go aside and learn who they are. Spend time with them. Ask many questions. Answer their questions. Be open and honest. Talk about a future together.

** CAUTION ** - You may not hug, kiss, or touch them in any way other than to hold their hands until instructed by us. Do not let lust cloud the love you MUST feel for them. The essence of our society must have love be the one and only foundation lest we become the wasteland of lust, desire, and moral degradation we were of centuries past.

When the time comes and BOTH feel their love for each other, one MUST ask the other to take their hand in marriage. This shouldn't be hard. It's what YOU WANT!!!! It's what they want. If they do not love you, then they may not take the ring. If they ask you and you do not love them, you cannot take their ring. You must continue to build the love until the exchange of rings. Failure to become engaged however will result in banishment from society. (That means you can't come to class the next week.) Banishment means that you may never marry. You will have no privileges in society. Society has no use for you. You will be sent to the islands of *Talasu Vorota.*

To prepare for this great and momentous time in your life, write a note to your future spouse. Let him or her know how you have prepared for this day. How you are eagerly awaiting them and how joyous the day will be.

Part Two:

One week after your engagement, you will celebrate *Lehfa Foo'eh* in an extravagant wedding and reception in your honor.

The Marriage Ceremony

(If the previous week went well and the "couples" have worked on developing their relationship, this scene will progress with ease. This scene requires preparation by those playing Tansley and Nadia to maintain the realism of the scene.)

Gurus Tansley and Nadia will join the betrothed couples in *Lehfa Foo'eh*. The following is the marriage ceremony.

"Welcome. <u>Man</u> and <u>Woman</u>, in the name of all that is holy, we gather today to bring two together so that they may be one. It is this ceremony that you, as Husband, Wife, and life partners will begin to share in all that has been given and will be given to you.

Through your expression of devotion to each other, you now freely and willingly enter into the state of matrimony. May you be strong and forthright in your resolve to make your marriage a peaceful place based on the foundation of love and commitment. Only through this can you live in harmonious bliss.

Soon you will recite The Vow of Love and Devotion. This is your solemn promise that you must not take lightly. This vow you make to each other goes beyond all promises. It is by these words that shall forever bind you as one soul. Yes, troubles will come, but it is this vow that will hold you strong against any storm. Your love is stronger than the force that binds the universe. Even death will not break it.

Your devotion is unwavering. Your spirits are now like birds upon the wind traveling to a new and distant land. So now, turn towards each other and take the hands of your life partner.

Man, repeat after me:

Woman, I have searched my soul and within it I have found you. You have lit the fire that shall forever give me warmth. Today, I take you as my life partner with excitement and with total devotion. My love shall never leave. It shall never stray. From this moment, my life is now yours. All I have I will share with you. I will protect you and love you even beyond the steps of death's door. This is my vow of love and devotion.

Woman repeat after me:

Man, I have searched my soul and within it I have found you. You are the light that leads my way. I am never lost when I am with you. Today, I take you as my life partner with excitement and with total devotion. My love shall never leave. It shall never stray. I take your life and give you mine. All I have I will share with you. I will serve you and love you even beyond the steps of death's door. This is my vow of love and devotion. This is my vow of love and devotion.

Having spoken the vows and pledged your love to each other, come forward and light your eternity candle. Through these two candles, let their fire join so that a new flame is created just as two souls have joined into one. Let this fire represent the flame that burns in your heart today and for always."

Each couple lights their fire, then steps aside.

"And now the exchanging of rings." (**Hand a ring to each groom**.) "Grooms, place this ring on the 3rd finger of your bride's left hand and repeat after me.

You are my love and my life. Forever and always."

Hand a ring to the brides. "Brides, place this ring on the 3rd finger of your groom's left hand and repeat after me.

You are my love and my life. Forever and always.

Now let me read the blessing.

Unknown to each
Somehow destiny did find
A common bond
Of their love, heart, and mind

A new journey
That these two ask now to seek
Filled with laughter
Love, devotion, and mystique

These two are one
With society's blessing
Their loving eyes
Be forever professing

By the saying of vows and the giving of rings, you are no longer two people, but are now one heart, one mind, and one soul. I now pronounce you life partners. May you live a life of peace and harmony. You may now kiss!"

RECEPTION

"Sharing of the champagne – It is tradition to share all things with your life partner. One of those is to share your first drink together. Take this cup and give it to your life partner that they may drink. Then they will give it to you to drink. It is also tradition that the one who drinks last, finishes the drink, lest it go to waste and bring bad luck to you."

"Cutting of the cake – The cake is also a symbol of sharing. We are more than two individuals joined as one. We are also a society joined together. Let this cake be shared amongst all as a symbol of our blessed society."

"The first dance – You have joined as life partners in your heart by your rings, and with your souls by the sharing of the drink. Now is the time to begin the sharing of your bodies. Take your partner and share this dance. Let your bodies also begin the journey."

Long Scene 9 - Gladiator games

Warning – Participate in this activity at your own risk. Neither Acting Up! or myself can be held liable for any bodily injury or property damage resulting from the use of this scene. A good stage combat course beforehand can be useful and will add realism.

Welcome to gladiator training! You were either captured by Roman forces and have been forced into being a gladiator, volunteered to be a gladiator in hopes of making money to help your family survive, or joined the ranks of gladiators for the fame that can come with it. (Pick one to base your character on.) Regardless of why you are here, the opportunity of success, riches, and most importantly, survival are open to you. Learn to fight, fight well, entertain Caesar and the Roman people, and you will be rewarded. Fight poorly and you will die in the Coliseum.

You will be trained here by Brutus Maximus, who killed more than 150 men and 1000 beasts in the arena during his gladiator days. Listen to all he and his assistants say. Your life will depend on it. Upon arrival, you will be required to take the Oath of the Gladiator. Gladiator trainees who refuse to take the oath or train diligently will be marked for especially cruel executions during the games.

Warning to Brutus and his assistants: Train them well or you'll be in the arena with them!!!!

After your period of training, you will be paired against another of your fellow gladiators for combat in the arena. If Caesar chooses to speak to either combatant before or during the match, any fighting must immediately stop. Both gladiators are to face Caesar, place their weapons on the ground, then kneel to Caesar until he orders you to rise.

Failure to follow these rules may result in your swift and immediate death.

For those who fight bravely, Caesar has offered up the following special rewards:

1. Land (A specially designated plaque in the new studio signifying you as the greatest gladiator.)
2. Money ($5 in real money)
3. Freedom (For the next two weeks, you will be able to choose which character you want to play from the ones available.)
4. A Wife (or Husband for our female gladiators) of your choice to be chosen from the ranks of the surviving gladiators. (For the not so swift people out there, this means that you can pick someone from class to be your spouse for a 30 period. Each week's following scenes will allow you to interact with that person as your spouse. That person will not be able to decline unless they won rewards 1-3, of which they will have to give you in exchange for their freedom.)

For those who disgrace the life of the gladiator by not taking the Oath, refusing to train, or fighting as a coward will be subjected to the following punishments (besides death):

1. Slavery (You will serve as Caesar's slave for a period of 21 days. That means you will do everything the Director says in class without complaint for the next three weeks of exercises.)
2. Prison (Your freedom will be severely reduced. You will be subjected to the smallest of roles for a period of 14 days.)
3. Loss of Citizenship (You will be allowed to remain in Rome, but your rights and privileges as a citizen will no longer apply for 21 days. This means any "marriages" or

"relationships" will be null and void. You may not interact with any people Caesar dictates during any class exercises until the time period is over.)

Gladiatorial Dress Requirements: Proper dress of all Romans and Gladiators is an absolute requirement. Visit the following sites to learn about proper dress code.

http://www.howtomakeatoga.info/

Further, all gladiators shall fight barefoot. You are to have a Roman name. Choose one and report it to trainer.

Enough with the setup and now to the warnings. The rewards and punishments are real. Obey the Golden Rule, stay in character, and you may be rewarded. Don't and the next few weeks of classes might not be a lot of fun. There are a limited number of rewards, but no limits to the number of punishments Caesar can give out. Consider this the motivation part.

During combat, you will use the weapons provided. Battles should not be over quickly, yet they should not linger. You are to entertain Caesar. He likes to be entertained. Asthmatics, bring your medicine!!! Weaklings, do some pushups and get in shape!! Be careful with the weapons. Caesar has spent a lot of money on adding golden statues to the palace and little was left over for good weapons. Break your weapon and you won't be able to easily defend yourself.

Caesar has spoken.

Long Scene 10 - Warsaw Ghetto

The one year anniversary is just two days away. You still remember the confusion and terror as the occupying Nazis forced you, your Jewish family, and your Jewish neighbors into this tiny apartment nearly a year ago. You are not alone however. Nearly the entire population of Warsaw has been forced into a tiny portion of the city. Conditions are deplorable. Food is scarce. Disease is rampant. You have already lost family members. Some have died already due to starvation. Some who went to work one day and never returned. Rumors are spreading that the Germans are deporting Polish Jews to extermination camps, but this is just a rumor. At least you hope it is.

Everything in Warsaw is controlled by the Nazi guards and the German Governor. Right now, the survival of you, your family, and friends is all that matters. Do whatever it takes to survive. Be willing to subject yourself to whatever the Germans want if it will help you or your family live. Some of you are lucky to be given occasional work to do, thereby earning food for your family. All able bodied men, women, and children are to report daily for food rations and work details. All citizens of Warsaw must obey the laws posted by the German high command and do so without question. Failure to do so may subject you to imprisonment or in the case of high offenses, death by firing squad.

NOTE - To prepare for the sensation of hunger, do not eat after lunch. Come to class hungry. Unless you're a Nazi. You can eat all you want. Bring a sandwich and eat in front of the "Jews" if you want.

Jewish adults must know what their trade was before the Nazi occupation. Choose from the following:

JEWS:
Men – carpenter, brick layer, machinist, baker, butcher, jeweler, dentist, barber, writer, painter
Women – seamstress, cleaning lady, baker, housewife, nurse, hair dresser

NAZIS:
Governor, Colonel, Lieutenant, Guards

To prepare for this scene we had a special movie night and watched *Schindler's List*. Besides being a great movie, it was invaluable in our studies of the relationships (some good/some bad) between the Nazis and the Jews.

More Long Form Scenes

The previous scenes I've listed are certainly not the only long scenes we have ever done. Over the course of one academic year, we performed 34 uniquely different scenes. At the end of the year we gave out our own "Academy Awards". We had the red carpet, paparazzi, and the winners all took home their own golden statues. Here are some of the other scenes we've done. If you use any of them, send me a note and let know how it went.

1. **Project Runaway** – They were divided into two teams. Each took a turn as a designer and then as a model. This is a lot of fun, but it makes a mess of the costume closet!

2. **Lost in Space** – They were divided into groups of 4 people then placed inside very cramped tents that served as our "spaceships". Each ship was placed out of earshot of the others, so that all communication was via walkie-talkie or text messages from Base Operations. During the course of the 90 minute exercise, various mechanical problems, medical emergencies, and alien attacks bombarded our space farers.

3. **1950s Sock Hop** – Need I say anymore? The costumes of the students were priceless.

4. **Woodstock** – Once again, little needs to be said about this, other than the fun I had playing Jimi Hendrix all night.

5. **Ski Lodge** – Sounds simple and lacking in creativity, but was an absolute blast. A real snowstorm was moving in to our quaint little town of Huntsville, Alabama, so we decided to treat it like we were snowed into our hotel in Aspen, Colorado. We turned off the lights to simulate the loss of electricity and joined in the "main lobby and bar" to enjoy the evening. A very casual setting that allowed each

person's character to interact on deeply personal levels with other characters.

6. **Prom/Hostage** – This scene won our writer's the award for best "Original Play" at our "Academy Awards". It started off very easy with the junior/senior prom but after two students were ridiculed by a group of teenage punk girls, things turned ugly. The ridiculed teens returned with guns and made the girls pay along with several innocent bystanders. Done properly, this scene will invoke fear unlike anything you will do.

7. **Shipwrecked** – AKA *"Lost"*, our survivors wake to find themselves stranded on what, at first, seems like a deserted island. Just finding supplies to survive is hard enough. Then there's the weather. (We make it rain inside our building.) Finally, our survivors find out they're not alone on this island and that certain people want them off of it immediately at any costs.

8. **Talent Show** – Your task is simple. Learn a song. Any song as long as it's at least 2:30 long then come in and either sing it with the accompanying music or lip-sync it. A very fun night for everyone.

9. **Reunion** – Everyone plays themselves, but its 10 years into the future. You've gathered back at your theater for a 10 year reunion. Oh, the stories you can tell.

10. **Family Reunion** – What better reason than to gather for the 80th birthday of your beloved grandmother. You've got cousins, their spouses, aunts, uncles, and even your eccentric old grandpa to catch up with. How long's it been since you saw them all? What have they been up to? A big banquet for everyone to partake from adds to the realism.

11. **Bellevue Hospital** – Winner of "Best Scene", "Best Actress", and "Best Supporting Actress" at our awards night, this was one of the most dynamic scenes we have ever done. I served as the doctor of the hospital with two nurses to help care for the "patients". Each student prepared an in depth back story as preparation for the class. The characters they created were beyond anything I could imagine. One girl sat at the front door and cried for the entire class as she "waited" for her family to come see her, even though they had "died" long ago. To this day, we have not brought this scene back for a redo because of the emotional toll it takes on all of us. So if you're looking for something really sad, then this is your scene.

12. **Prison** – This takes some preparation time, but is a highly effective scene. You can choose to keep everyone in a common area or you can "build" individual cells, which is what we did. This allowed us to more easily monitor the "inmates". You'll need someone to be the warden and a few people to play the guards. Our guard's personalities and levels of professionalism were very different. We had an inept guard. One who was very disciplined, but not cruel. And one who was quite sadistic and took great pleasure in seeing an inmate "suffer". As for our "inmates", they too ran the spectrum of personalities. Some were very obedient. Others not so. We had one who would regularly try to escape (Best Supporting Actor) whenever the inept guard got distracted. We had inmates who had a relationship with another inmate. Some were friends. Some were enemies. This isn't a scene that can be done quickly. We let it run for a full two hours.

I cannot stress enough how important it is to properly prepare your characters each week. And don't fall into the trap of preparing a similar character each week. It becomes very easy to always play the little kid, or the really tough guy, or even the shy, hide-in-the-corner character. The great thing about acting is "living" lives of people who are not us. How fun it is to be an astronaut, or gun slinger, or a hippie from the 60s. You greater your diversity of characters, the greater your acting skills will grow.

For the stage manager, set decorator, and prop master… As with any long form scene, the preparation time you take to properly set up the scene, will pay off handsomely in the end. The more you give the actors to work with, the more real the scene will be to them. Sometimes it might only take 30 minutes, but other times such as in our case, my production manager and I have spent as much as 8 hours of scene preparation. (It takes a long time to build a prison or create a realistic island.) Give them what they need so that they can give the audience what they need. Realism! For all of us involved at the theater, we should be giving all we have to our art. Taking short cuts helps no one. Remember Golden Rule #1:

Make your scene partner look good!

They're counting on you to do your very best. And you're counting on them. Acting isn't a solo act. It is as much a team effort as any sport. Don't let your team down.

Chapter 19

Continuing the Journey

I hope this book has been helpful to you. It is certainly not an all-inclusive study into acting. I don't believe any book can ever achieve that. Keep in mind that acting requires more than just studying it from a book. It requires a commitment to the stage. If we are to hone our craft to our full potential, we have to step on the stage and practice. If you've taken the time to read this book in its entirety, then you are a committed to perfecting your art. If you haven't already, now is the time for you to seek out a teacher that can build from the knowledge you've gained here. If you are building your own theater troupe, take this book and use it as your foundation. To all of you I wish you the best of luck. Get out there a break a leg! I know the task before you is daunting, but the reward is great. For all of my actors and directors out there, I am here to help you. Please drop me a line or call the theater and I would be more than willing to pass on any wisdom I have, be it ever so slight.

Kevin Meier
c/o Acting Up! Academy of Dramatic Arts
8402 B Whitesburg Drive
Huntsville, AL 35802
(256) 270-9636
actingup@knology.net

Further Reading

Sanford Meisner on Acting, Sanford Meisner and Dennis Longwell

Improvisation for the Theater: A Handbook of Teaching and Directing Techniques, Viola Spolin

Improvisation Starters: *A Collection of 900 Improvisation Situations for the Theater*, Philip Bernardi

Bibliography

Silverberg, Larry. *The Sanford Meisner Approach, Workbook One: An Actor's Workbook,* Smith & Kraus Pub Inc, 1994

Silverberg, Larry. *The Sanford Meisner Approach, Workbook Two, Emotional Freedom.* Smith & Kraus Pub Inc, 1997.

Silverberg, Larry. *The Sanford Meisner Approach, Workbook Three, Tackling the Text.* Smith & Kraus Pub Inc, 1998.

Silverberg, Larry. *The Sanford Meisner Approach, Workbook Four, Playing the Part.* Smith & Kraus Pub Inc, 2000.

Dr. Seuss. *Green Eggs and Ham*, Beginner Books, 1960

Fulton, Thomas Q. "THE ACTOR'S OATH by Thomas Q. Fulton, Jr." *Tom Fulton, Actor, Director, Teacher, Executive Director - The Fairmount Center.* Tom Fulton, 2005. Web. <http://www.tomfulton.com/oath.htm>.

Theilke, Janet. "A 1945 Code of Ethics for Theatre Workers Surfaces." *LA STAGE TIMES.* LA Stage Times, 11 Aug. 2009. Web. <http://www.lastagetimes.com/2009/08/a-1945-code-of-ethics-for-theatre-workers-surfaces/>.

About the Author

Kevin Meier is the founder, co-owner, and artistic director of Acting Up! Academy of Dramatic Arts located in Huntsville, Alabama. A student of Kirk Baltz (*Dances with Wolves*), he has been actively involved in theater and film for over 40 years; acting, dancing, directing, designing, writing, and producing throughout the United States including the stage versions of *Willy Wonka and the Chocolate Factory, Little Mermaid, Around the World in 80 Days, Death by Chocolate, Conflict,* and many, many more. He has worked on over a dozen films, including *Constellation, The Shelter, St. Joseph College,* and *The Telephone Calls*. Kevin is also a founding member of the improvisational Christian comedy group, Potters Clay. His newest improv troupe, The Nuclear ReActors, entertain people throughout the southeast with their own brand of high energy, out-of-the-box humor. Kevin has been teaching the Sanford Meisner to children and adults for over a decade. He is well known for his enthusiasm, dedication, and limitless energy.

13283909R00105

Made in the USA
Lexington, KY
25 January 2012